Certified Kubernetes Security Specialist (CKS) Study Guide
In-Depth Guidance and Practice

Benjamin Muschko

Beijing · Boston · Farnham · Sebastopol · Tokyo

Certified Kubernetes Security Specialist (CKS) Study Guide

by Benjamin Muschko

Copyright © 2023 Automated Ascent, LLC. All rights reserved.

Published by O'Reilly Media, Inc., 1005 Gravenstein Highway North, Sebastopol, CA 95472.

O'Reilly books may be purchased for educational, business, or sales promotional use. Online editions are also available for most titles (*https://oreilly.com*). For more information, contact our corporate/institutional sales department: 800-998-9938 or *corporate@oreilly.com*.

Acquisitions Editor: John Devins
Development Editor: Michele Cronin
Production Editor: Beth Kelly
Copyeditor: Liz Wheeler
Proofreader: Amnet Systems, LLC

Indexer: Potomac Indexing, LLC
Interior Designer: David Futato
Cover Designer: Karen Montgomery
Illustrator: Kate Dullea

June 2023:   First Edition

Revision History for the First Edition
2023-06-08:   First Release

See *https://oreilly.com/catalog/errata.csp?isbn=9781098132972* for release details.

The O'Reilly logo is a registered trademark of O'Reilly Media, Inc. *Certified Kubernetes Security Specialist (CKS) Study Guide*, the cover image, and related trade dress are trademarks of O'Reilly Media, Inc.

978-1-098-13297-2

[LSI]

Table of Contents

Preface

The Kubernetes certification program has been around since 2018, or five years as of this writing. During this time, security has become more and more important everywhere, including the Kubernetes world. Recently, the role of Certified Kubernetes Security Specialist (CKS) (*https://www.cncf.io/certification/cks*) has been added to the certification track to address the need. Security can have different facets, and the way you address those concerns can be very diverse. That's where the Kubernetes ecosystem comes into play. Apart from Kubernetes built-in security features, many tools have evolved that help with identifying and fixing security risks. As a Kubernetes administrator, you need to be familiar with the wide range of concepts and tools to harden your clusters and applications.

The CKS certification program was created to verify competence on security-based topics, and it requires a successful pass of the Certified Kubernetes Administrator (CKA) (*https://www.cncf.io/certification/cka*) exam before you can register. If you are completely new to the Kubernetes certification program, then I would recommend exploring the CKA or Certified Kubernetes Application Developer (CKAD) (*https://www.cncf.io/certification/ckad*) program first.

In this study guide, I will explore the topics covered in the CKS exam to fully prepare you to pass the certification exam. We'll look at determining when and how you should apply the core concepts of Kubernetes and external tooling to secure cluster components, cluster configuration, and applications running in a Pod. I will also offer tips to help you better prepare for the exam and share my personal experience with getting ready for all aspects of it.

The CKS is different from the typical multiple-choice format of other certifications. It's completely performance based and requires you to demonstrate deep knowledge of the tasks at hand under immense time pressure. Are you ready to pass the test on the first go?

Who This Book Is For

This book is for anyone who already passed the CKA exam and wants to broaden their knowledge in the realm of security. Given that you need to pass the CKA exam before signing up for the CKS, you should already be familiar with the format of the exam questions and environment. Chapter 1 only briefly recaps the general aspects of the exam curriculum, but it highlights the information specific to the CKS exam. If you have not taken the CKA exam yet, I recommend taking a step by reading the *Certified Kubernetes Administrator (CKA) Study Guide* (O'Reilly). The book will provide you with the foundation you need to get started with the CKS.

What You Will Learn

The content of the book condenses the most important aspects relevant to the CKS exam. Cloud-provider-specific Kubernetes implementations like AKS or GKE do not need to be considered. Given the plethora of configuration options available in Kubernetes, it's almost impossible to cover all use cases and scenarios without duplicating the official documentation. Test takers are encouraged to reference the Kubernetes documentation (*https://kubernetes.io/docs/home*) as the go-to compendium for broader exposure. External tools relevant to the CKS exam, such as Trivy or Falco, are only covered on a high level. Refer to their documentation to explore more features, functionality, and configuration options.

Structure of This Book

The outline of the book follows the CKS curriculum to a T. While there might be a more natural, didactical structure for learning Kubernetes in general, the curriculum outline will help test takers prepare for the exam by focusing on specific topics. As a result, you will find yourself cross-referencing other chapters of the book depending on your existing knowledge level.

Be aware that this book covers only the concepts relevant to the CKS exam. Foundational Kubernetes concepts and primitives are not discussed. Refer to the Kubernetes documentation or other books if you want to dive deeper.

Practical experience with Kubernetes is key to passing the exam. Each chapter contains a section named "Sample Exercises" with practice questions. Solutions to those questions can be found in the Appendix.

Conventions Used in This Book

The following typographical conventions are used in this book:

Italic

Indicates new terms, URLs, and email addresses.

`Constant width`

Used for filenames, file extensions, and program listings, as well as within paragraphs to refer to program elements such as variable or function names, databases, data types, environment variables, statements, and keywords.

`Constant width bold`

Shows commands or other text that should be typed literally by the user.

 This element signifies a tip or suggestion.

 This element signifies a general note.

 This element indicates a warning or caution.

Using Code Examples

Some code snippets in the book use the backslash character (\) to break up a single line into multiple lines to make it fit the page. You will need to rectify the code manually if you are copy-pasting it directly from the book content to a terminal or editor. The better choice is to refer to the code book's GitHub repository (*https://github.com/bmuschko/cks-study-guide*), which already has the proper formatting.

The GitHub repository is distributed under the Apache License 2.0. The code is free to use in commercial and open source projects. If you encounter an issue in the source code or if you have a question, open an issue in the GitHub issue tracker (*https://oreil.ly/YTRzJ*). I'll be happy to have a conversation and fix any issues that might arise.

This book is here to help you get your job done. In general, if example code is offered with this book, you may use it in your programs and documentation. You do not need to contact us for permission unless you're reproducing a significant portion of the code. For example, writing a program that uses several chunks of code from this book does not require permission. Selling or distributing examples from O'Reilly books does require permission. Answering a question by citing this book and quoting example code does not require permission. Incorporating a significant amount of example code from this book into your product's documentation does require permission. We appreciate, but generally do not require, attribution. An attribution usually includes the title, author, publisher, and ISBN. For example: "*Certified Kubernetes Security Specialist (CKS) Study Guide* by Benjamin Muschko (O'Reilly). Copyright 2023 Automated Ascent, LLC, 978-1-098-13297-2."

If you feel your use of code examples falls outside fair use or the permission given above, feel free to contact us at *permissions@oreilly.com*.

O'Reilly Online Learning

 For more than 40 years, *O'Reilly Media* has provided technology and business training, knowledge, and insight to help companies succeed.

Our unique network of experts and innovators share their knowledge and expertise through books, articles, and our online learning platform. O'Reilly's online learning platform gives you on-demand access to live training courses, in-depth learning paths, interactive coding environments, and a vast collection of text and video from O'Reilly and 200+ other publishers. For more information, visit *http://oreilly.com*.

How to Contact Us

Please address comments and questions concerning this book to the publisher:

O'Reilly Media, Inc.
1005 Gravenstein Highway North
Sebastopol, CA 95472
800-889-8969 (in the United States or Canada)
707-829-7019 (international or local)
707-829-0104 (fax)
support@oreilly.com
https://www.oreilly.com/about/contact.html

We have a web page for this book, where we list errata, examples, and any additional information. You can access this page at *https://oreil.ly/cks-study-guide*.

For news and information about our books and courses, visit *http://oreilly.com*.

Find us on LinkedIn: *https://linkedin.com/company/oreilly-media*

Follow us on Twitter: *http://twitter.com/oreillymedia*

Watch us on YouTube: *http://youtube.com/oreillymedia*

Follow the author on Twitter: *https://twitter.com/bmuschko*

Follow the author on GitHub: *https://github.com/bmuschko*

Follow the author's blog: *https://bmuschko.com*

Acknowledgments

Every book project is a long journey and would not be possible without the help of the editorial staff and technical reviewers. Special thanks go to Robin Smorenburg, Werner Dijkerman, Michael Kehoe, and Liz Rice for their detailed technical guidance and feedback. I would also like to thank the editors at O'Reilly Media, John Devins and Michele Cronin, for their continued support and encouragement.

CHAPTER 1

Exam Details and Resources

This introductory chapter addresses the most pressing questions candidates ask when preparing for the Certified Kubernetes Security Specialist (CKS) exam (*https://www.cncf.io/certification/cks*). We will discuss the target audience for the certification, the curriculum, and the exam environment, as well as tips and tricks and additional learning resources. If you're already familiar with the certification program, you can directly jump to any of the chapters covering the technical concepts.

Kubernetes Certification Learning Path

The CNCF offers four different Kubernetes certifications. Figure 1-1 categorizes each of them by target audience. You will find that the CKS is the most advanced certification you can acquire. It is the only one with a prerequisite of passing another certification first; all others are standalone programs.

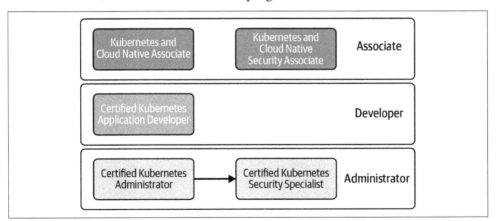

Figure 1-1. Kubernetes certifications learning path

Let's have a very brief look at the details for each certification to see if the CKS is the right fit for you.

Kubernetes and Cloud Native Associate (KCNA)

KCNA is an entry-level certification program for anyone interested in cloud-native application development, runtime environments, and tooling. While the exam does cover Kubernetes, it does *not* expect you to actually solve problems in a practical manner. This exam is suitable for candidates interested in the topic with a broad exposure to the ecosystem.

Kubernetes and Cloud Native Security Associate (KCSA)

The certification focuses on basic knowledge of security concepts and their application in a Kubernetes cluster. The breadth and depth of the program is comparable to the KCNA, as it does not require solving problems hands-on.

Certified Kubernetes Application Developer (CKAD)

The CKAD exam focuses on verifying your ability to build, configure, and deploy a microservices-based application to Kubernetes. You are not expected to actually implement an application; however, the exam is suitable for developers familiar with topics like application architecture, runtimes, and programming languages.

Certified Kubernetes Administrator (CKA)

The target audience for the CKA exam are DevOps practitioners, system administrators, and site reliability engineers. This exam tests your ability to perform in the role of a Kubernetes administrator, which includes tasks like cluster, network, storage, and beginner-level security management, with a big emphasis on troubleshooting scenarios.

Certified Kubernetes Security Specialist (CKS)

The CKS exam expands on the topics verified by the CKA exam. Passing the CKA is a prerequisite before you can even sign up for the CKS exam. For this certification, you are expected to have a deeper knowledge of Kubernetes security aspects. The curriculum covers topics like applying best practices for building containerized applications and ensuring a secure Kubernetes runtime environment.

Exam Objectives

Vulnerabilities in software and IT infrastructure, if exploited, can pose a major threat to organizations. The Cloud Native Computing Foundation (CNCF) developed the Certified Kubernetes Security Specialist (CKS) certification to verify a Kubernetes administrator's proficiency to protect a Kubernetes cluster and the cloud native software operated in it. As part of the CKS exam, you are expected to understand Kubernetes core security features, as well as third-party tools and established practices for securing applications and infrastructure.

Kubernetes version used during the exam

At the time of writing, the exam is based on Kubernetes 1.26. All content in this book will follow the features, APIs, and command-line support for that specific version. It's certainly possible that future versions will break backward compatibility. While preparing for the certification, review the Kubernetes release notes (*https://oreil.ly/u3REo*) and practice with the Kubernetes version used during the exam to avoid unpleasant surprises.

In this book, I am going to explain each of the security threats by providing a specific use case. We'll start by talking about a scenario that allows an attacker to gain access to a cluster, inject malicious code, or use a vulnerability to hack into the system. Then, we'll touch on the concepts, practices, and/or tools that will prevent that situation. With this approach, you'll be able to evaluate the severity of a security risk and the need for implementing security measures.

Curriculum

The following overview lists the high-level sections, also called domains, of the CKS exam and their scoring weights:

- 10%: Cluster Setup
- 15%: Cluster Hardening
- 15%: System Hardening
- 20%: Minimize Microservice Vulnerabilities
- 20%: Supply Chain Security
- 20%: Monitoring, Logging, and Runtime Security

How the book works

The outline of the book follows the CKS curriculum to a T. While there might be a more natural, didactical organization structure to learn Kubernetes in general, the curriculum outline will help test takers prepare for the exam by focusing on specific topics. As a result, you will find yourself cross-referencing other chapters of the book depending on your existing knowledge level.

Let's break down each domain in detail in the next sections.

Cluster Setup

This section covers Kubernetes concepts that have already been covered by the CKA exam; however, they assume that you already understand the basics and expect you to be able to go deeper. Here, you will be tested on network policies and their effects on disallowing and granting network communication between Pods within the same namespace and across multiple namespaces. The main focus will be on restricting communication to minimize the attack surface. Furthermore, the domain "cluster setup" will verify your knowledge of setting up an Ingress object with Transport Layer Security (TLS) termination.

A big emphasis lies on identifying and fixing security vulnerabilities by inspecting the cluster setup. External tools like kube-bench can help with automating the process. As a result of executing the tool against your cluster, you will receive an actionable list of vulnerabilities. Changing the configuration settings of your cluster according to the recommendations can help with significantly reducing the security risk.

Last, locking down cluster node endpoints, ports, and graphical user interfaces (GUIs) can help with making it harder for attackers to gain control of the cluster. You need to be aware of the default cluster settings so that you can limit access to them as much as possible. Kubernetes binaries and executables like kubectl, kubeadm, and the kubelet need to be checked against their checksum to ensure they haven't been tampered with by a third party. You need to understand how to retrieve the checksum file for binaries and how to use it verify the validity of the executable.

Cluster Hardening

Most organizations start out with a cluster that allows developers and administrators alike to manage the Kubernetes installation, configuration, and management of any objects. While this is a convenient approach for teams getting comfortable with Kubernetes, it is not a safe and sound situation, as it poses the potential of opening the floodgates for attackers. Once access has been gained to the cluster, any malicious operation can be performed.

Role-based access control (RBAC) maps permissions to users or processes. The exam requires deep knowledge of the API resources involved. The domain "cluster hardening" also focuses the topic of keeping the cluster version up-to-date to ensure the latest bug fixes are picked up. Kubernetes exposes the API server via endpoints. You should be aware of strategies for minimizing its exposure to the outside world.

System Hardening

This domain is all about understanding how to minimize access to the host system and external network to reduce the attack surface. This is where OS-level tools like AppArmor and seccomp come into play. You will need to demonstrate their use to fulfill the requirement. The domain also touches on the use of AWS IAM roles for clusters running in Amazon's cloud environment specifically.

Minimize Microservice Vulnerabilities

Security contexts define privilege and access control for containers. Platform and security teams can govern and enforce desired security measures on the organizational level. The exam requires you to understand Pod security policies and the OPA Gatekeeper for that purpose. Moreover, you'll be asked to demonstrate defining Secrets of different types and consuming them from Pods to inject sensitive runtime information.

Sometimes, you may want to experiment with container images from an unverified source or a potentially unsafe origin. Container runtime sandboxes like gVisor and Kata Containers can be configured in Kubernetes to execute a container image with very restricted permissions. Configuring and using such a container runtime sandbox is part of this domain. Further, you need to be aware of the benefits of mTLS Pod-to-Pod encryption and how to configure it.

Supply Chain Security

Container security starts with the base image. You need to be aware of the best practices for building container images that minimize the risk of introducing security vulnerabilities from the get-go. Optimally, you will only allow pulling trusted container images from an organization-internal container registry that has already scanned the image for vulnerabilities before it can be used. Allowing only those registries is paramount and will be one of the topics important to this domain. Tools like Trivy can help with the task of scanning images for vulnerabilities and are listed as a requirement to pass the exam.

Monitoring, Logging, and Runtime Security

One of the focus points of this domain is behavior analytics, the process of observing abnormal and malicious events. Falco is the primary tool to get familiar with in this section. A container should not be mutable after it has been started to avoid opening additional backdoors for attackers. You will need to be aware of best practices and demonstrate the ability to apply them in the configuration of a container.

Audit logging can be helpful for a real-time view on cluster events or for debugging purposes. Configuring audit logging for a Kubernetes cluster is part of the exam.

Involved Kubernetes Primitives

Some of the exam objectives can be covered by understanding the relevant core Kubernetes primitives. It is to be expected that the exam combines multiple concepts in a single problem. Refer to Figure 1-2 as a rough guide to the applicable Kubernetes resources and their relationships.

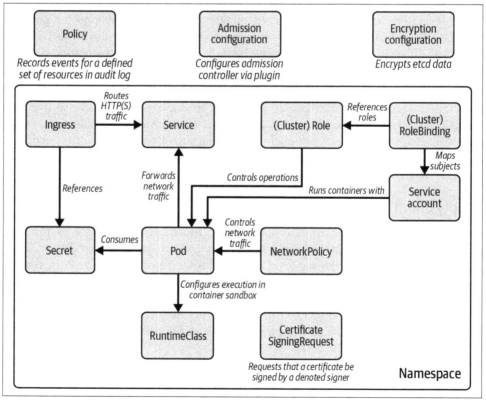

Figure 1-2. Kubernetes primitives relevant to the exam

In addition to Kubernetes core primitives, you will also need to have a grasp of specific Custom Resource Definitions (CRDs) provided by open source projects. For example, the Open Policy Agent (OPA) Gatekeeper provides the primitives' ConstraintTemplate.

Involved External Tools

A significant portion of the exam requires you to demonstrate expertise with external, security-related tools. Some of the tools have been spelled out explicitly in the curriculum, but there are other tools that fall into the same functional category. At the very least, you will have to be familiar with the following tools:

- kube-bench (*https://oreil.ly/y3mbO*)
- AppArmor (*https://apparmor.net*)
- seccomp (*https://oreil.ly/vxdZV*)
- gVisor (*https://gvisor.dev*)
- Kata Containers (*https://oreil.ly/vmCZH*)
- Trivy (*https://oreil.ly/RsWka*)
- Falco (*https://oreil.ly/LGT8B*)

Documentation

During the exam, you are permitted to open a well-defined list of web pages as a reference. You can freely browse those pages and copy-paste code in the exam terminal. The Frequently Asked Questions (FAQ) (*https://oreil.ly/ZcKNf*) for the CKS spells out a list of permitted URLs.

The official Kubernetes documentation includes the reference manual, the GitHub site, and the blog:

- Reference manual: *https://kubernetes.io/docs*
- GitHub: *https://github.com/kubernetes*
- Blog: *https://kubernetes.io/blog*

For external tools, you are allowed to open and browse the following URL:

- Trivy: *https://github.com/aquasecurity/trivy*
- Falco: *https://falco.org/docs*
- AppArmor: *https://gitlab.com/apparmor/apparmor/-/wikis/Documentation*

Candidate Skills

The CKS certification assumes that you already have an administrator-level understanding of Kubernetes. The CNCF requires you to acquire the CKA certificate as a prerequisite. Without those credentials, you won't be able to sign up for the CKS exam. If you have not passed the CKA exam yet or if you want to brush up on the topics, I'd recommend having a look at my book *Certified Kubernetes Administrator (CKA) Study Guide*.

For the remainder of the book, I will simply assume that you already have the knowledge needed for the CKA. Therefore, I won't repeat the basics on overlapping topics anymore. For convenience reasons, I will point you to the relevant information in the CKA book as needed. Please revisit the sections on the exam environment and time management in the CKA book. They equally apply to the CKS exam.

Practicing and Practice Exams

Hands-on practice is extremely important when it comes to passing the exam. For that purpose, you'll need a functioning Kubernetes cluster environment. The following options stand out:

- I found it useful to run one or many virtual machines using Vagrant (*https://oreil.ly/2jLJS*) and VirtualBox (*https://oreil.ly/3BhDj*). Those tools help with creating an isolated Kubernetes environment that is easy to bootstrap and dispose on demand. Some of the practice exercises in this book use this setup as their starting point.

- It is relatively easy to install a simple Kubernetes cluster on your developer machine. The Kubernetes documentation provides various installation options (*https://oreil.ly/JrBUh*), depending on your operating system. Minikube is useful when it comes to experimenting with more advanced features like Ingress or storage classes, as it provides the necessary functionality as add-ons that can be installed with a single command.

- If you're a subscriber to the O'Reilly learning platform (*https://oreil.ly/xOtTT*), you have unlimited access to labs running a Kubernetes environment (*https://oreil.ly/gYiVj*). In addition, you can test your knowledge with the help of the CKS practice test in the form of interactive labs (*https://oreil.ly/9Jp6j*).

You may also want to try one of the following commercial learning and practice resources:

- The book *Certified Kubernetes Administrator (CKA) Study Guide* covers the curriculum of the CKA certification. Revisit the book's materials for a refresher on the foundations.

- Killer Shell (*https://killer.sh*) is a simulator with sample exercises for all Kubernetes certifications.

- The CKS practice exam from Study4exam (*https://oreil.ly/c3Y7_*) offers a commercial, web-based test environment to assess your knowledge level.

Summary

The CKS exam verifies your hands-on knowledge of security-related aspects in Kubernetes. You are expected to understand core Kubernetes primitives and concepts that can fulfill security requirements, such as RBAC, network policies, and Ingress. The exam also involves helpful third-party security tools. You need to demonstrate how to effectively use those tools. Passing the CKA exam is mandatory for the CKS. Make sure you pass the CKA first if you haven't done so yet.

The following chapters align with the exam curriculum so that you can map the content to the learning objectives. At the end of each chapter, you will find sample exercises to practice your knowledge. The discussion of each domain concludes with a short summary of the most important aspects to learn.

CHAPTER 2

Cluster Setup

The first domain of the exam deals with concerns related to Kubernetes cluster setup and configuration. In this chapter, we'll only drill into the security-specific aspects and not the standard responsibilities of a Kubernetes administrator.

At a high level, this chapter covers the following concepts:

- Using network policies to restrict Pod-to-Pod communication
- Running CIS benchmark tooling to identify security risks for cluster components
- Setting up an Ingress object with TLS support
- Protecting node ports, API endpoints, and GUI access
- Verifying platform binaries against their checksums

Using Network Policies to Restrict Pod-to-Pod Communication

For a microservice architecture to function in Kubernetes, a Pod needs to be able to reach another Pod running on the same or on a different node without Network Address Translation (NAT). Kubernetes assigns a unique IP address to every Pod upon creation from the Pod CIDR range of its node. The IP address is ephemeral and therefore cannot be considered stable over time. Every restart of a Pod leases a new IP address. It's recommended to use Pod-to-Service communication over Pod-to-Pod communication so that you can rely on a consistent network interface.

The IP address assigned to a Pod is unique across all nodes and namespaces. This is achieved by assigning a dedicated subnet to each node when registering it. When creating a new Pod on a node, the IP address is leased from the assigned subnet. This is handled by the Container Network Interface (CNI) plugin. As a result, Pods on a node can communicate with all other Pods running on any other node of the cluster.

Network policies act similarly to firewall rules, but for Pod-to-Pod communication. Rules can include the direction of network traffic (ingress and/or egress) for one or many Pods within a namespace or across different namespaces, as well as their targeted ports. For a deep-dive coverage on the basics of network policies, refer to the book *Certified Kubernetes Application Developer (CKAD) Study Guide* (O'Reilly) or the Kubernetes documentation (*https://oreil.ly/WChde*). The CKS exam primarily focuses on restricting cluster-level access with network policies.

Defining the rules of network policies correctly can be challenging. The page networkpolicy.io provides a visual editor for network policies that renders a graphical representation in the browser.

Scenario: Attacker Gains Access to a Pod

Say you are working for a company that operates a Kubernetes cluster with three worker nodes. Worker node 1 currently runs two Pods as part of a microservices architecture. Given Kubernetes default behavior for Pod-to-Pod network communication, Pod 1 can talk to Pod 2 unrestrictedly and vice versa.

As you can see in Figure 2-1, an attacker gained access to Pod 1. Without defining network policies, the attacker can simply talk to Pod 2 and cause additional damage. This vulnerability isn't restricted to a single namespace. Pods 3 and 4 can be reached and compromised as well.

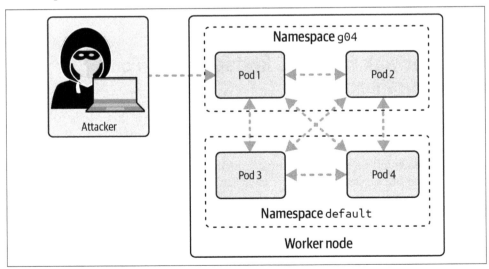

Figure 2-1. An attacker who gained access to Pod 1 has network access to other Pods

Observing the Default Behavior

We'll set up three Pods to demonstrate the unrestricted Pod-to-Pod network communication in practice. As you can see in Example 2-1, the YAML manifest defines the Pods named `backend` and `frontend` in the namespace `g04`. The `other` Pod lives in the `default` namespace. Observe the label assignment for the namespace and Pods. We will reference them a little bit later in this chapter when defining network policies.

Example 2-1. YAML manifest for three Pods in different namespaces

```
apiVersion: v1
kind: Namespace
metadata:
  labels:
    app: orion
  name: g04
---
apiVersion: v1
kind: Pod
metadata:
  labels:
    tier: backend
  name: backend
  namespace: g04
spec:
  containers:
  - image: bmuschko/nodejs-hello-world:1.0.0
    name: hello
    ports:
    - containerPort: 3000
  restartPolicy: Never
---
apiVersion: v1
kind: Pod
metadata:
  labels:
    tier: frontend
  name: frontend
  namespace: g04
spec:
  containers:
  - image: alpine
    name: frontend
    args:
    - /bin/sh
    - -c
    - while true; do sleep 5; done;
  restartPolicy: Never
---
apiVersion: v1
```

```
kind: Pod
metadata:
  labels:
    tier: outside
  name: other
spec:
  containers:
  - image: alpine
    name: other
    args:
    - /bin/sh
    - -c
    - while true; do sleep 5; done;
  restartPolicy: Never
```

Start by creating the objects from the existing YAML manifest using the declarative kubectl apply command:

```
$ kubectl apply -f setup.yaml
namespace/g04 created
pod/backend created
pod/frontend created
pod/other created
```

Let's verify that the namespace g04 runs the correct Pods. Use the -o wide CLI option to determine the virtual IP addresses assigned to the Pods. The backend Pod uses the IP address 10.0.0.43, and the frontend Pod uses the IP address 10.0.0.193:

```
$ kubectl get pods -n g04 -o wide
NAME           READY   STATUS    RESTARTS   AGE   IP           NODE        \
  NOMINATED NODE   READINESS GATES
backend        1/1     Running   0          15s   10.0.0.43    minikube  \
  <none>           <none>
frontend       1/1     Running   0          15s   10.0.0.193   minikube  \
  <none>           <none>
```

The default namespace handles a single Pod:

```
$ kubectl get pods
NAME    READY   STATUS    RESTARTS   AGE
other   1/1     Running   0          4h45m
```

The frontend Pod can talk to the backend Pod as no communication restrictions have been put in place:

```
$ kubectl exec frontend -it -n g04 -- /bin/sh
/ # wget --spider --timeout=1 10.0.0.43:3000
Connecting to 10.0.0.43:3000 (10.0.0.43:3000)
remote file exists
/ # exit
```

The other Pod residing in the `default` namespace can communicate with the back end Pod without problems:

```
$ kubectl exec other -it -- /bin/sh
/ # wget --spider --timeout=1 10.0.0.43:3000
Connecting to 10.0.0.43:3000 (10.0.0.43:3000)
remote file exists
/ # exit
```

In the next section, we'll talk about restricting Pod-to-Pod network communication to a maximum level with the help of deny-all network policy rules. We'll then open up ingress and/or egress communication only for the kind of network communication required for the microservices architecture to function properly.

Denying Directional Network Traffic

The best way to restrict Pod-to-Pod network traffic is with the principle of least privilege. Least privilege means that Pods should communicate with the lowest privilege for network communication. You'd usually start by disallowing traffic in any direction and then opening up the traffic needed by the application architecture.

The Kubernetes documentation (*https://oreil.ly/PZOGf*) provides a couple of helpful YAML manifest examples. Example 2-2 shows a network policy that denies ingress traffic to all Pods in the namespace g04.

Example 2-2. A default deny-all ingress network policy

```
apiVersion: networking.k8s.io/v1
kind: NetworkPolicy
metadata:
  name: default-deny-ingress
  namespace: g04
spec:
  podSelector: {}
  policyTypes:
  - Ingress
```

Selecting all Pods is denoted by the value {} assigned to the `spec.podSelector` attribute. The value attribute `spec.policyTypes` defines the denied direction of traffic. For incoming traffic, you can add `Ingress` to the array. Outgoing traffic can be specified by the value `Egress`. In this particular example, we disallow all ingress traffic. Egress traffic is still permitted.

The contents of the "deny-all" network policy have been saved in the file deny-all-ingress-network-policy.yaml. The following command creates the object from the file:

```
$ kubectl apply -f deny-all-ingress-network-policy.yaml
networkpolicy.networking.k8s.io/default-deny-ingress created
```

Let's see how this changed the runtime behavior for Pod-to-Pod network communication. The frontend Pod cannot talk to the backend Pod anymore, as observed by running the same wget command we used earlier. The network call times out after one second, as defined by the CLI option --timeout:

```
$ kubectl exec frontend -it -n g04 -- /bin/sh
/ # wget --spider --timeout=1 10.0.0.43:3000
Connecting to 10.0.0.43:3000 (10.0.0.43:3000)
wget: download timed out
/ # exit
```

Furthermore, Pods running in a different namespace cannot connect to the backend Pod anymore either. The following wget command makes a call from the other Pod running in the default namespace to the IP address of the backend Pod:

```
$ kubectl exec other -it -- /bin/sh
/ # wget --spider --timeout=1 10.0.0.43:3000
Connecting to 10.0.0.43:3000 (10.0.0.43:3000)
wget: download timed out
```

This call times out as well.

Allowing Fine-Grained Incoming Traffic

Network policies are additive. To grant more permissions for network communication, simply create another network policy with more fine-grained rules. Say we wanted to allow ingress traffic to the backend Pod only from the frontend Pod that lives in the same namespace. Ingress traffic from all other Pods should be denied independently of the namespace they are running in.

Network policies heavily work with label selection to define rules. Identify the labels of the g04 namespace and the Pod objects running in the same namespace so we can use them in the network policy:

```
$ kubectl get ns g04 --show-labels
NAME    STATUS   AGE    LABELS
g04     Active   12m    app=orion,kubernetes.io/metadata.name=g04
$ kubectl get pods -n g04 --show-labels
NAME       READY   STATUS    RESTARTS   AGE      LABELS
backend    1/1     Running   0          9m46s    tier=backend
frontend   1/1     Running   0          9m46s    tier=frontend
```

The label assignment for the namespace g04 includes the key-value pair app=orion. The Pod backend label set includes the key-value pair tier=backend, and the front end Pod the key-value pair tier=frontend.

Create a new network policy that allows the frontend Pod to talk to the backend Pod only on port 3000. No other communication should be allowed. The YAML manifest representation in Example 2-3 shows the full network policy definition.

Example 2-3. Network policy that allows ingress traffic

```
apiVersion: networking.k8s.io/v1
kind: NetworkPolicy
metadata:
  name: backend-ingress
  namespace: g04
spec:
  podSelector:
    matchLabels:
      tier: backend
  policyTypes:
  - Ingress
  ingress:
  - from:
    - namespaceSelector:
        matchLabels:
          app: orion
      podSelector:
        matchLabels:
          tier: frontend
    ports:
    - protocol: TCP
      port: 3000
```

The definition of the network policy has been stored in the file backend-ingress-network-policy.yaml. Create the object from the file:

```
$ kubectl apply -f backend-ingress-network-policy.yaml
networkpolicy.networking.k8s.io/backend-ingress created
```

The frontend Pod can now talk to the backend Pod:

```
$ kubectl exec frontend -it -n g04 -- /bin/sh
/ # wget --spider --timeout=1 10.0.0.43:3000
Connecting to 10.0.0.43:3000 (10.0.0.43:3000)
remote file exists
/ # exit
```

Pods running outside of the g04 namespace still can't connect to the backend Pod. The wget command times out:

```
$ kubectl exec other -it -- /bin/sh
/ # wget --spider --timeout=1 10.0.0.43:3000
Connecting to 10.0.0.43:3000 (10.0.0.43:3000)
wget: download timed out
```

Applying Kubernetes Component Security Best Practices

Managing an on-premises Kubernetes cluster gives you full control over the configuration options applied to cluster components, such as the API server, etcd, the kubelet, and others. It's not uncommon to simply go with the default configuration settings used by kubeadm when creating the cluster nodes. Some of those default settings may expose cluster components to unnecessary attack opportunities.

Hardening the security measures of a cluster is a crucial activity for any Kubernetes administrator seeking to minimize attack vectors. You can either perform this activity manually if you are aware of the best practices, or use an automated process.

The Center for Internet Security (CIS) (*https://www.cisecurity.org*) is a not-for-profit organization that publishes cybersecurity best practices. Part of their best practices portfolio is the Kubernetes CIS Benchmark (*https://oreil.ly/CUe_D*), a catalog of best practices for Kubernetes environments. You will find a detailed list of recommended security settings for cluster components on their web page.

CIS benchmarking for cloud provider Kubernetes environments

The Kubernetes CIS Benchmark is geared toward a self-managed installation of Kubernetes. Cloud provider Kubernetes environments, such as Amazon Elastic Kubernetes Service (EKS) and Google Kubernetes Engine (GKE), provide a managed control plane accompanied by their own command line tools. Therefore, the security recommendations made by the Kubernetes CIS Benchmark may be less fitting. Some tools, like kube-bench, discussed next, provide verification checks specifically for cloud providers.

Using kube-bench

You can use the tool kube-bench (*https://oreil.ly/y3mbO*) to check Kubernetes cluster components against the CIS Benchmark best practices in an automated fashion. Kube-bench can be executed in a variety of ways. For example, you can install it as a platform-specific binary in the form of an RPM or Debian file. The most convenient and direct way to run the verification process is by running kube-bench in a Pod directly on the Kubernetes cluster. For that purpose, create a Job object with the help of a YAML manifest checked into the GitHub repository of the tool.

Start by creating the Job from the file `job-master.yaml`, or `job-node.yaml` depending on whether you want to inspect a control plane node or a worker node. The following command runs the verification checks against the control plane node:

```
$ kubectl apply -f https://raw.githubusercontent.com/aquasecurity/kube-bench/\
main/job-master.yaml
job.batch/kube-bench-master created
```

Upon Job execution, the corresponding Pod running the verification process can be identified by its name in the `default` namespace. The Pod's name starts with the prefix `kube-bench`, then appended with the type of the node plus a hash at the end. The following output uses the Pod named `kube-bench-master-8f6qh`:

```
$ kubectl get pods
NAME                        READY   STATUS      RESTARTS   AGE
kube-bench-master-8f6qh     0/1     Completed   0          45s
```

Wait until the Pod transitions into the "Completed" status to ensure that all verification checks have finished. You can have a look at the benchmark result by dumping the logs of the Pod:

```
$ kubectl logs kube-bench-master-8f6qh
```

Sometimes, it may be more convenient to write the verification results to a file. You can redirect the output of the `kubectl logs` command to a file, e.g., with the command `kubectl logs kube-bench-master-8f6qh > control-plane-kube-bench-results.txt`.

The kube-bench Verification Result

The produced verification result can be lengthy and detailed, but it consists of these key elements: the type of the inspected node, the inspected components, a list of passed checks, a list of failed checks, a list of warnings, and a high-level summary:

```
[INFO] 1 Control Plane Security Configuration ❶
[INFO] 1.1 Control Plane Node Configuration Files
[PASS] 1.1.1 Ensure that the API server pod specification file permissions are \
set to 644 or more restrictive (Automated) ❷
...
[INFO] 1.2 API Server
[WARN] 1.2.1 Ensure that the --anonymous-auth argument is set to false \
(Manual) ❸
...
[FAIL] 1.2.6 Ensure that the --kubelet-certificate-authority argument is set \
as appropriate (Automated) ❹

== Remediations master ==
...
1.2.1 Edit the API server pod specification file /etc/kubernetes/manifests/ \
kube-apiserver.yaml on the control plane node and set the below parameter.
--anonymous-auth=false
```

```
...
1.2.6 Follow the Kubernetes documentation and setup the TLS connection between ❺
the apiserver and kubelets. Then, edit the API server pod specification file ❺
/etc/kubernetes/manifests/kube-apiserver.yaml on the control plane node and \ ❺
set the --kubelet-certificate-authority parameter to the path to the cert \ ❺
file for the certificate authority. ❺
--kubelet-certificate-authority=<ca-string> ❺


...
== Summary total == ❻
42 checks PASS
9 checks FAIL
11 checks WARN
0 checks INFO
```

❶ The inspected node, in this case the control plane node.

❷ A passed check. Here, the file permissions of the API server configuration file.

❸ A warning message that prompts you to manually check the value of an argument provided to the API server executable.

❹ A failed check. For example, the flag `--kubelet-certificate-authority` should be set for the API server executable.

❺ The remediation action to take to fix a problem. The number, e.g., 1.2.1, of the failure or warning corresponds to the number assigned to the remediation action.

❻ The summary of all passed and failed checks plus warning and informational messages.

Fixing Detected Security Issues

The list of reported warnings and failures can be a bit overwhelming at first. Keep in mind that you do not have to fix them all at once. Some checks are merely guidelines or prompts to verify an assigned value for a configuration. The following steps walk you through the process of eliminating a warning message.

The configuration files of the control plane components can be found in the directory /etc/kubernetes/manifests on the host system of the control plane node. Say you wanted to fix the warning 1.2.12 reported by kube-bench:

```
[INFO] 1.2 API Server
...
[WARN] 1.2.12 Ensure that the admission control plugin AlwaysPullImages is \
set (Manual)
```

```
== Remediations master ==
...
1.2.12 Edit the API server pod specification file /etc/kubernetes/manifests/ \
kube-apiserver.yaml
on the control plane node and set the --enable-admission-plugins parameter \
to include AlwaysPullImages.
--enable-admission-plugins=...,AlwaysPullImages,...
```

As proposed by the remediation action, you are supposed to edit the configuration file for the API server and add the value AlwaysPullImages to the list of admission plugins. Go ahead and edit the file kube-apiserver.yaml:

$ sudo vim /etc/kubernetes/manifests/kube-apiserver.yaml

After appending the value AlwaysPullImages to the argument --enable-admission-plugins, the result could look as follows:

```
apiVersion: v1
kind: Pod
metadata:
  annotations:
    kubeadm.kubernetes.io/kube-apiserver.advertise-address.endpoint: \
    192.168.56.10:6443
  creationTimestamp: null
  labels:
    component: kube-apiserver
    tier: control-plane
  name: kube-apiserver
  namespace: kube-system
spec:
  containers:
  - command:
    - kube-apiserver
    - --advertise-address=192.168.56.10
    - --allow-privileged=true
    - --authorization-mode=Node,RBAC
    - --client-ca-file=/etc/kubernetes/pki/ca.crt
    - --enable-admission-plugins=NodeRestriction,AlwaysPullImages
...
```

Save the changes to the file. The Pod running the API server in the kube-system namespace will be restarted automatically. The startup process can take a couple of seconds. Therefore, executing the following command may take a while to succeed:

```
$ kubectl get pods -n kube-system
NAME                          READY   STATUS    RESTARTS   AGE
...
kube-apiserver-control-plane  1/1     Running   0          71m
...
```

You will need to delete the existing Job object before you can verify the changed result:

```
$ kubectl delete job kube-bench-master
job.batch "kube-bench-master" deleted
```

The verification check 1.2.12 now reports a passed result:

```
$ kubectl apply -f https://raw.githubusercontent.com/aquasecurity/kube-bench/\
main/job-master.yaml
job.batch/kube-bench-master created
$ kubectl get pods
NAME                      READY    STATUS      RESTARTS   AGE
kube-bench-master-5gjdn   0/1      Completed   0          10s
$ kubectl logs kube-bench-master-5gjdn | grep 1.2.12
[PASS] 1.2.12 Ensure that the admission control plugin AlwaysPullImages is \
set (Manual)
```

Creating an Ingress with TLS Termination

An Ingress routes HTTP and/or HTTPS traffic from outside of the cluster to one or many Services based on a matching URL context path. You can see its functionality in action in Figure 2-2.

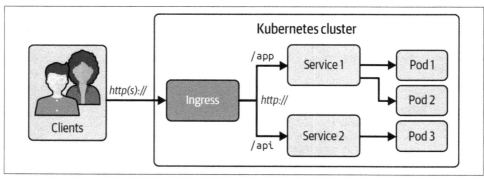

Figure 2-2. Managing external access to the Services via HTTP(S)

The Ingress has been configured to accept HTTP and HTTPS traffic from outside of the cluster. If the caller provides the context path /app, then the traffic is routed to Service 1. If the caller provides the context path /api, then the traffic is routed to Service 2. It's important to point out that the communication typically uses unencrypted HTTP network communication as soon as it passes the Ingress.

Given that the Ingress API resource is a part of the CKAD and CKA exam, we are not going to discuss the basics anymore here. For a detailed discussion, refer to the information in the *Certified Kubernetes Administrator (CKA) Study Guide* or the Kubernetes documentation (*https://oreil.ly/wmk2s*).

The role of an Ingress controller

Remember that an Ingress cannot work without an Ingress controller. The Ingress controller evaluates the collection of rules defined by an Ingress that determine traffic routing. One example of a production-grade Ingress controller is the F5 NGINX Ingress Controller (*https://oreil.ly/jOo6P*) or AKS Application Gateway Ingress Controller (*https://oreil.ly/ckuqf*). You can find other options listed in the Kubernetes documentation (*https://oreil.ly/BXx8e*). If you are using minikube, make sure to enable the Ingress add-on (*https://oreil.ly/11QAA*).

The primary focus of the CKS lies on setting up Ingress objects with TLS termination. Configuring the Ingress for HTTPS communication relieves you from having to deal with securing the network communication on the Service level. In this section of the book, you will learn how to create a TLS certificate and key, how to feed the certificate and key to a TLS-typed Secret object, and how to configure an Ingress object so that it supports HTTPS communication.

Setting Up the Ingress Backend

In the context of an Ingress, a *backend* is the combination of Service name and port. Before creating the Ingress, we'll take care of the Service, a Deployment, and the Pods running nginx so we can later on demonstrate the routing of HTTPS traffic to an actual application. All of those objects are supposed to exist in the namespace t75. Example 2-4 defines all of those resources in a single YAML manifest file setup.yaml as a means to quickly create the Ingress backend.

Example 2-4. YAML manifest for exposing nginx through a Service

```
apiVersion: v1
kind: Namespace
metadata:
  name: t75
---
apiVersion: apps/v1
kind: Deployment
metadata:
  name: nginx-deployment
  namespace: t75
  labels:
    app: nginx
spec:
  replicas: 3
  selector:
    matchLabels:
      app: nginx
```

```
    template:
      metadata:
        labels:
          app: nginx
      spec:
        containers:
        - name: nginx
          image: nginx:1.14.2
          ports:
          - containerPort: 80
---
apiVersion: v1
kind: Service
metadata:
  name: accounting-service
  namespace: t75
spec:
  selector:
    app: nginx
  ports:
  - protocol: TCP
    port: 80
    targetPort: 80
```

Create the objects from the YAML file with the following command:

```
$ kubectl apply -f setup.yaml
namespace/t75 created
deployment.apps/nginx-deployment created
service/accounting-service created
```

Let's quickly verify that the objects have been created properly, and the Pods have transitioned into the "Running" status. Upon executing the get all command, you should see a Deployment named nginx-deployment that controls three replicas, and a Service named accounting-service of type ClusterIP:

```
$ kubectl get all -n t75
NAME                                      READY   STATUS    RESTARTS   AGE
pod/nginx-deployment-6595874d85-5rdrh     1/1     Running   0          108s
pod/nginx-deployment-6595874d85-jmhvh     1/1     Running   0          108s
pod/nginx-deployment-6595874d85-vtwxp     1/1     Running   0          108s

NAME                          TYPE        CLUSTER-IP      EXTERNAL-IP   PORT(S) \
  AGE
service/accounting-service    ClusterIP   10.97.101.228   <none>        80/TCP \
  108s

NAME                               READY   UP-TO-DATE   AVAILABLE   AGE
deployment.apps/nginx-deployment   3/3     3            3           108s
```

Calling the Service endpoint from another Pod running on the same node should result in a successful response from the nginx Pod. Here, we are using the `wget` command to verify the behavior:

```
$ kubectl run tmp --image=busybox --restart=Never -it --rm \
  -- wget 10.97.101.228:80
Connecting to 10.97.101.228:80 (10.97.101.228:80)
saving to 'index.html'
index.html              100% |**|   612  0:00:00 ETA
'index.html' saved
pod "tmp" deleted
```

With those objects in place and functioning as expected, we can now concentrate on creating an Ingress with TLS termination.

Creating the TLS Certificate and Key

We will need to generate a TLS certificate and key before we can create a TLS Secret. To do this, we will use the OpenSSL command. The resulting files are named `accounting.crt` and `accounting.key`:

```
$ openssl req -nodes -new -x509 -keyout accounting.key -out accounting.crt \
  -subj "/CN=accounting.tls"
Generating a 2048 bit RSA private key
.........................+
.........................+
writing new private key to 'accounting.key'
-----
$ ls
accounting.crt accounting.key
```

For use in production environments, you'd generate a key file and use it to obtain a TLS certificate from a certificate authority (CA). For more information on creating a TLS certification and key, see the OpenSSL documentation (*https://oreil.ly/sETSb*).

Creating the TLS-Typed Secret

The easiest way to create a Secret is with the help of an imperative command. This method of creation doesn't require you to manually base64-encode the certificate and key values. The encoding happens automatically upon object creation. The following command uses the Secret option `tls` and assigns the certificate and key file name with the options `--cert` and `--key`:

```
$ kubectl create secret tls accounting-secret --cert=accounting.crt \
  --key=accounting.key -n t75
secret/accounting-secret created
```

Example 2-5 shows the YAML representation of a TLS Secret if you want to create the object declaratively.

Example 2-5. A Secret using the type `kubernetes.io/tls`

```
apiVersion: v1
kind: Secret
metadata:
  name: accounting-secret
  namespace: t75
type: kubernetes.io/tls
data:
  tls.crt: LS0tLS1CRUdJTiBDRVJUSUZJQ0FURS0tLS0tCk...
  tls.key: LS0tLS1CRUdJTiBQUklWQVRFIEtFWS0tLS0tCk...
```

Make sure to assign the values for the attributes `tls.crt` and `tls.key` as single-line, base64-encoded values. To produce the base64-encoded value, simply point the `base64` command to the file name you want to convert the contents for. The following example base64-encoded the contents of the file `accounting.crt`:

```
$ base64 accounting.crt
LS0tLS1CRUdJTiBDRVJUSUZJQ0FURS0tLS0tCk1JSUNyakNC...
```

Creating the Ingress

You can use the imperative method to create the Ingress with the help of a one-liner command shown in the following snippet. Crafting the value of the `--rule` argument is hard to get right. You will likely have to refer to the `--help` option for the `create ingress` command as it requires a specific expression. The information relevant to creating the connection between Ingress object and the TLS Secret is the appended argument `tls=accounting-secret`:

```
$ kubectl create ingress accounting-ingress \
  --rule="accounting.internal.acme.com/*=accounting-service:80, \
  tls=accounting-secret" -n t75
ingress.networking.k8s.io/accounting-ingress created
```

Example 2-6 shows a YAML representation of an Ingress. The attribute for defining the TLS information is `spec.tls[]`.

Example 2-6. A YAML manifest for defining a TLS-terminated Ingress

```
apiVersion: networking.k8s.io/v1
kind: Ingress
metadata:
  name: accounting-ingress
  namespace: t75
spec:
  tls:
  - hosts:
    - accounting.internal.acme.com
    secretName: accounting-secret
```

```
  rules:
  - host: accounting.internal.acme.com
    http:
      paths:
      - path: /
        pathType: Prefix
        backend:
          service:
            name: accounting-service
            port:
              number: 80
```

After creating the Ingress object with the imperative or declarative approach, you should be able to find it in the namespace t75. As you can see in the following output, the port 443 is listed in the "PORT" column, indicating that TLS termination has been enabled:

```
$ kubectl get ingress -n t75
NAME                    CLASS   HOSTS                          ADDRESS         \
   PORTS       AGE
accounting-ingress      nginx   accounting.internal.acme.com   192.168.64.91 \
   80, 443     55s
```

Describing the Ingress object shows that the backend could be mapped to the path / and will route traffic to the Pod via the Service named accounting-service:

```
$ kubectl describe ingress accounting-ingress -n t75
Name:             accounting-ingress
Labels:           <none>
Namespace:        t75
Address:          192.168.64.91
Ingress Class:    nginx
Default backend:  <default>
TLS:
  accounting-secret terminates accounting.internal.acme.com
Rules:
  Host                          Path  Backends
  ----                          ----  --------
  accounting.internal.acme.com
                                /     accounting-service:80 \
                                (172.17.0.5:80,172.17.0.6:80,172.17.0.7:80)
Annotations:                    <none>
Events:
  Type    Reason  Age            From                       Message
  ----    ------  ----           ----                       -------
  Normal  Sync    1s (x2 over 31s)  nginx-ingress-controller  Scheduled for sync
```

Calling the Ingress

To test the behavior on a local Kubernetes cluster on your machine, you need to first find out the IP address of a node. The following command reveals the IP address in a minikube environment:

```
$ kubectl get nodes -o wide
NAME       STATUS   ROLES          AGE     VERSION    INTERNAL-IP     \
  EXTERNAL-IP   OS-IMAGE                KERNEL-VERSION   CONTAINER-RUNTIME
minikube   Ready    control-plane   3d19h   v1.24.1    192.168.64.91 \
  <none>        Buildroot 2021.02.12    5.10.57          docker://20.10.16
```

Next, you'll need to add the IP address to the hostname mapping to your /etc/hosts file:

```
$ sudo vim /etc/hosts
...
192.168.64.91   accounting.internal.acme.com
```

You can now send HTTPS requests to the Ingress using the assigned domain name and receive an HTTP response code 200 in return:

```
$ wget -O- https://accounting.internal.acme.com --no-check-certificate
--2022-07-28 15:32:43--  https://accounting.internal.acme.com/
Resolving accounting.internal.acme.com (accounting.internal.acme.com)... \
192.168.64.91
Connecting to accounting.internal.acme.com (accounting.internal.acme.com) \
|192.168.64.91|:443... connected.
WARNING: cannot verify accounting.internal.acme.com's certificate, issued \
by 'CN=Kubernetes Ingress Controller Fake Certificate,O=Acme Co':
  Self-signed certificate encountered.
WARNING: no certificate subject alternative name matches
        requested host name 'accounting.internal.acme.com'.
HTTP request sent, awaiting response... 200 OK
```

Protecting Node Metadata and Endpoints

Kubernetes clusters expose ports used to communicate with cluster components. For example, the API server uses the port 6443 by default to enable clients like kubectl to talk to it when executing commands.

The Kubernetes documentation lists those ports in "Ports and Protocols" (*https://oreil.ly/iN993*). The following two tables show the default port assignments per node.

Table 2-1 shows the default inbound ports on the cluster node.

Table 2-1. Inbound control plane node ports

Port range	Purpose
6643	Kubernetes API server
2379–2380	etcd server client API
10250	Kubelet API
10259	kube-scheduler
10257	kube-controller-manager

Many of those ports are configurable. For example, you can modify the API server port by providing a different value with the flag `--secure-port` in the configuration file */etc/kubernetes/manifests/kube-apiserver.yaml*, as documented (*https://oreil.ly/TTzAz*) for the cluster component. For all other cluster components, please refer to their corresponding documentation.

Table 2-2 lists the default inbound ports on a worker node.

Table 2-2. Inbound worker node ports

Port range	Purpose
10250	Kubelet API
30000–32767	NodePort Services

To secure the ports used by cluster components, set up firewall rules to minimize the attack surface area. For example, you could decide not to expose the API server to anyone outside of the intranet. Clients using `kubectl` would only be able to run commands against the Kubernetes cluster if logged into the VPN, making the cluster less vulnerable to attacks.

Cloud provider Kubernetes clusters (e.g., on AWS, Azure, or Google Cloud) expose so-called metadata services. Metadata services are APIs that can provide sensitive data like an authentication token for consumption from VMs or Pods without any additional authorization. For the CKS exam, you need to be aware of those node endpoints and cloud provider metadata services. Furthermore, you should have a high-level understanding of how to protect them from unauthorized access.

Scenario: A Compromised Pod Can Access the Metadata Server

Figure 2-3 shows an attacker who gained access to a Pod running on a node within a cloud provider Kubernetes cluster.

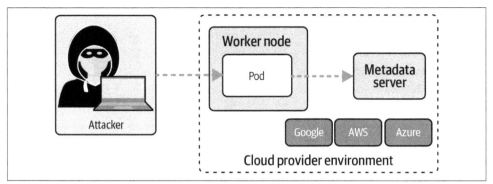

Figure 2-3. An attacker who gained access to the Pod has access to metadata server

Access to the metadata server has not been restricted in any form. The attacker can retrieve sensitive information, which could open other possibilities of intrusion.

Protecting Metadata Server Access with Network Policies

Let's pick one of the cloud providers that exposes a metadata endpoint. In AWS, the metadata server can be reached with the IP address 169.254.169.254, as described in the AWS documentation (*https://oreil.ly/6DsIx*). The endpoints exposed can provide access to EC2 instance metadata. For example, you can retrieve the local IP address of an instance to manage a connection to an external application or to contact the instance with the help of a script. See the corresponding documentation page (*https:// oreil.ly/Bwdej*) for calls to those endpoints made with the curl command line tool.

To prevent any Pod in a namespace from reaching the IP address of the metadata server, set up a network policy that allows egress traffic to all IP addresses except 169.254.169.254. Example 2-7 demonstrates a YAML manifest with such a rule set.

Example 2-7. A default deny-all egress to IP address 169.254.169.254 network policy

```
apiVersion: networking.k8s.io/v1
kind: NetworkPolicy
metadata:
  name: default-deny-egress-metadata-server
  namespace: a12
spec:
  podSelector: {}
  policyTypes:
  - Egress
  egress:
  - to:
    - ipBlock:
        cidr: 0.0.0.0/0
```

```
      except:
      - 169.254.169.254/32
```

Once the network policy has been created, Pods in the namespace a12 should not be able to reach the metadata endpoints anymore. For detailed examples that use the endpoints via curl, see the relevant AWS documentation (*https://oreil.ly/fQ07b*).

Protecting GUI Elements

The kubectl tool isn't the only user interface (UI) for managing a cluster. While kubectl allows for fine-grained operations, most organizations prefer a more convenient graphical user interface (GUI) for managing the objects of a cluster. You can choose from a variety of options. The Kubernetes Dashboard (*https://oreil.ly/ABDQo*) is a free, web-based application. Other GUI dashboards for Kubernetes like Portainer (*https://oreil.ly/i_FJv*) go beyond the basic functionality by adding tracing of events or visualizations of hardware resource consumption. In this section, we'll focus on the Kubernetes Dashboard as it is easy to install and configure.

Scenario: An Attacker Gains Access to the Dashboard Functionality

The Kubernetes Dashboard runs as a Pod inside of the cluster. Installing the Dashboard also creates a Service of type ClusterIP that only allows access to the endpoint from within the cluster. To make the Dashboard accessible to end users, you'd have to expose the Service outside of the cluster. For example, you could switch to a NodePort Service type or stand up an Ingress. Figure 2-4 illustrates the high-level architecture of deploying and accessing the Dashboard.

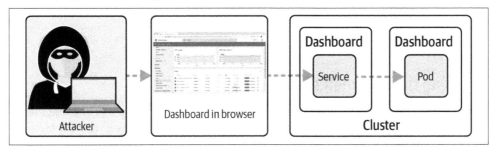

Figure 2-4. An attacker who gained access to the Dashboard

As soon as you expose the Dashboard to the outside world, attackers can potentially gain access to it. Without the right security settings, objects can be deleted, modified, or used for malicious purposes. The most prominent victim of such an attack was Tesla, which in 2018 fell prey to hackers who gained access to its unprotected Dashboard to mine cryptocurrencies. Since then, newer versions of the Dashboard changed default settings to make it more secure from the get-go.

Installing the Kubernetes Dashboard

Installing the Kubernetes Dashboard is straightforward. You can create the relevant objects with the help of the YAML manifest available in the project's GitHub repository. The following command installs all necessary objects:

```
$ kubectl apply -f https://raw.githubusercontent.com/kubernetes/dashboard/\
v2.6.0/aio/deploy/recommended.yaml
```

Rendering metrics in Dashboard

You may also want to install the metrics server (*https://oreil.ly/ 3Rtkl*) if you are interested in inspecting resource consumption metrics as part of the Dashboard functionality.

You can find the objects created by the manifest in the kubernetes-dashboard namespace. Among them are Deployments, Pods, and Services. The following command lists all of them:

```
$ kubectl get deployments,pods,services -n kubernetes-dashboard
NAME                                      READY   UP-TO-DATE   AVAILABLE   AGE
deployment.apps/dashboard-metrics-scraper  1/1     1            1           11m
deployment.apps/kubernetes-dashboard       1/1     1            1           11m

NAME                                         READY   STATUS    RESTARTS   AGE
pod/dashboard-metrics-scraper-78dbd9dbf5-f8z4x 1/1   Running   0          11m
pod/kubernetes-dashboard-5fd5574d9f-ns7nl      1/1   Running   0          11m

NAME                             TYPE        CLUSTER-IP      EXTERNAL-IP \
   PORT(S)      AGE
service/dashboard-metrics-scraper ClusterIP  10.98.6.37      <none>      \
   8000/TCP     11m
service/kubernetes-dashboard      ClusterIP  10.102.234.158  <none>      \
   80/TCP       11m
```

Accessing the Kubernetes Dashboard

The kubectl proxy command can help with temporarily creating a proxy that allows you to open the Dashboard in a browser. This functionality is only meant for troubleshooting purposes and is not geared toward production environments. You can find information about the proxy command in the documentation (*https://oreil.ly/gGsqX*):

```
$ kubectl proxy
Starting to serve on 127.0.0.1:8001
```

Open the browser with the URL *http://localhost:8001/api/v1/namespaces/kubernetes-dashboard/services/https:kubernetes-dashboard:/proxy*. The Dashboard will ask you to provide an authentication method and credentials. The recommended way to configure the Dashboard is through bearer tokens.

Creating a User with Administration Privileges

Before you can authenticate in the login screen, you need to create a ServiceAccount and ClusterRoleBinding object that grant admin permissions. Start by creating the file admin-user-serviceaccount.yaml and populate it with the contents shown in Example 2-8.

Example 2-8. Service account for admin permissions

```
apiVersion: v1
kind: ServiceAccount
metadata:
  name: admin-user
  namespace: kubernetes-dashboard
```

Next, store the contents of Example 2-9 in the file admin-user-clusterrole binding.yaml to map the ClusterRole named cluster-admin to the ServiceAccount.

Example 2-9. ClusterRoleBinding for admin permissions

```
apiVersion: rbac.authorization.k8s.io/v1
kind: ClusterRoleBinding
metadata:
  name: admin-user
roleRef:
  apiGroup: rbac.authorization.k8s.io
  kind: ClusterRole
  name: cluster-admin
subjects:
- kind: ServiceAccount
  name: admin-user
  namespace: kubernetes-dashboard
```

Create both objects with the following declarative command:

```
$ kubectl create -f admin-user-serviceaccount.yaml
serviceaccount/admin-user created
$ kubectl create -f admin-user-clusterrolebinding.yaml
clusterrolebinding.rbac.authorization.k8s.io/admin-user created
```

You can now create the bearer token of the admin user with the following command. The command will generate a token for the provided ServiceAccount object and render it on the console:

```
$ kubectl create token admin-user -n kubernetes-dashboard
eyJhbGciOiJSUzI1NiIsImtpZCI6...
```

Expiration of a service account token

By default, this token will expire after 24 hours. That means that the token object will be deleted automatically once the "time to live" (TTL) has passed. You can change the TTL of a token by providing the command line option `--ttl`. For example, a value of `40h` will expire the token after 40 hours. A value of `0` indicates that the token should never expire.

Copy the output of the command and paste it into the "Enter token" field of the login screen, as shown in Figure 2-5.

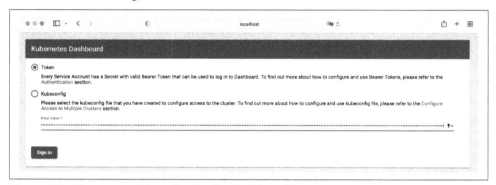

Figure 2-5. The usage of the token in the Dashboard login screen

Pressing the "Sign in" button will bring you to the Dashboard shown in Figure 2-6.

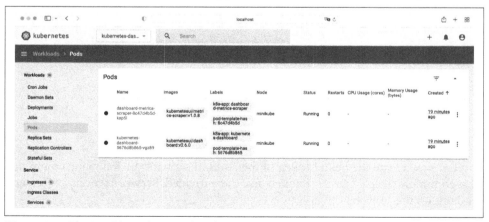

Figure 2-6. The Dashboard view of Pods in a specific namespace

You can now manage end user and cluster objects without any restrictions.

Creating a User with Restricted Privileges

In the previous section, you learned how to create a user with cluster-wide administrative permissions. Most users of the Dashboard only need a restricted set of permissions, though. For example, developers implementing and operating cloud-native applications will likely only need a subset of administrative permissions to perform their tasks on a Kubernetes cluster. Creating a user for the Dashboard with restricted privileges consists of a three-step approach:

1. Create a ServiceAccount object.
2. Create a ClusterRole object that defines the permissions.
3. Create a ClusterRoleBinding that maps the ClusterRole to the ServiceAccount.

As you can see, the process is very similar to the one we went through for the admin user. Step 2 is new, as we need to be specific about which permissions we want to grant. The YAML manifests that follow will model a user working as a developer that should only be allowed read-only permissions (e.g., getting, listing, and watching resources).

Start by creating the file `restricted-user-serviceaccount.yaml` and populate it with the contents shown in Example 2-10.

Example 2-10. Service account for restricted permissions

```
apiVersion: v1
kind: ServiceAccount
metadata:
  name: developer-user
  namespace: kubernetes-dashboard
```

The ClusterRole in Example 2-11 only allows getting, listing, and watching resources. All other operations are not permitted. Store the contents in the file `restricted-user-clusterrole.yaml`.

Example 2-11. ClusterRole for restricted permissions

```
apiVersion: rbac.authorization.k8s.io/v1
kind: ClusterRole
metadata:
  annotations:
    rbac.authorization.kubernetes.io/autoupdate: "true"
  name: cluster-developer
rules:
- apiGroups:
  - '*'
  resources:
```

```
    - '*'
  verbs:
  - get
  - list
  - watch
- nonResourceURLs:
    - '*'
  verbs:
  - get
  - list
  - watch
```

Last, map the ServiceAccount to the ClusterRole in the file `restricted-user-clusterrolebinding.yaml`, as shown in Example 2-12.

Example 2-12. ClusterRoleBinding for restricted permissions

```
apiVersion: rbac.authorization.k8s.io/v1
kind: ClusterRoleBinding
metadata:
  name: developer-user
roleRef:
  apiGroup: rbac.authorization.k8s.io
  kind: ClusterRole
  name: cluster-developer
subjects:
- kind: ServiceAccount
  name: developer-user
  namespace: kubernetes-dashboard
```

Create all objects with the following declarative command:

```
$ kubectl create -f restricted-user-serviceaccount.yaml
serviceaccount/restricted-user created
$ kubectl create -f restricted-user-clusterrole.yaml
clusterrole.rbac.authorization.k8s.io/cluster-developer created
$ kubectl create -f restricted-user-clusterrolebinding.yaml
clusterrolebinding.rbac.authorization.k8s.io/developer-user created
```

Generate the bearer token of the restricted user with the following command:

```
$ kubectl create token developer-user -n kubernetes-dashboard
eyJhbGciOiJSUzI1NiIsImtpZCI6...
```

Operations that are not allowed for the logged-in user will not be rendered as disabled options in the GUI. You can still select the option; however, an error message is rendered. Figure 2-7 illustrates the behavior of the Dashboard if you try to delete a Pod via the user that doesn't have the permissions to perform the operation.

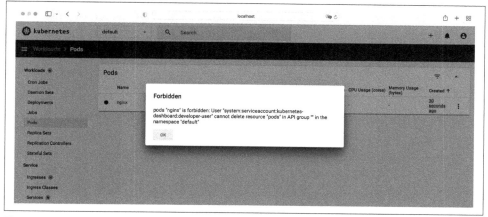

Figure 2-7. An error message rendered when trying to invoke a permitted operation

Avoiding Insecure Configuration Arguments

Securing the Dashboard in production environments involves the usage of execution arguments (*https://oreil.ly/gS1hE*) necessary for properly configuring authentication and authorization. By default, login functionality is enabled and the HTTPS endpoint will be exposed on port 8443. You can provide TLS certificates with the `--tls-cert-file` and `--tls-cert-key` command line options if you don't want them to be auto-generated.

Avoid setting the command line arguments `--insecure-port` to expose an HTTP endpoint and `--enable-insecure-login` to enable serving the login page over HTTP instead of HTTPS. Furthermore, make sure you *don't* use the option `--enable-skip-login` as it would allow circumventing an authentication method by simply clicking a Skip button in the login screen.

Verifying Kubernetes Platform Binaries

The Kubernetes project publishes client and server binaries with every release. The client binary refers to the executable `kubectl`. Server binaries include `kubeadm`, as well as the executable for the API server, the scheduler, and the kubelet. You can find those files under the "tags" sections of the Kubernetes GitHub repository (*https://oreil.ly/vHpAV*) or on the release page at *https://dl.k8s.io*.

Scenario: An Attacker Injected Malicious Code into Binary

The executables `kubectl` and `kubeadm` are essential for interacting with Kubernetes. `kubectl` lets you run commands against the API server, e.g., for managing objects. `kubeadm` is necessary for upgrading cluster nodes from one version to another. Say you are in the process of upgrading the cluster version (*https://oreil.ly/hTJ57*) from 1.23 to 1.24. As part of the process, you will need to upgrade the kubeadm binary as well. The official upgrade documentation is very specific about what commands to use for upgrading the binary.

Say an attacker managed to modify the kubeadm executable for version 1.24 and coaxed you into thinking that you need to download that very binary from a location where the malicious binary was placed. As shown in Figure 2-8, you'd expose yourself to running malicious code every time you invoke the modified kubeadm executable. For example, you may be sending credentials to a server outside of your cluster, which would open new ways to infiltrate your Kubernetes environment.

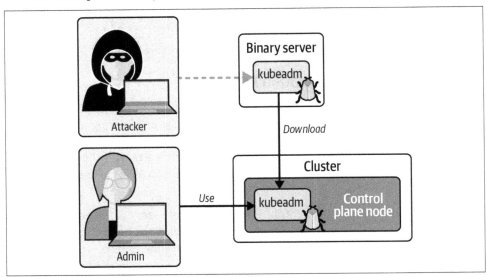

Figure 2-8. An attacker who injected malicious code into a binary

Verifying a Binary Against Hash

You can verify the validity of a binary with the help of a hash code like MD5 or SHA. Kubernetes publishes SHA256 hash codes for each binary. You should run through a hash validation for individual binaries before using them for the first time. Should the generated hash code not match with the one you downloaded, then there's something off with the binary. The binary may have been modified by a third party or you didn't use the hash code for the correct binary type or version.

You can download the corresponding hash code for a binary from *https://dl.k8s.io*. The full URL for a hash code reflects the version, operating system, and architecture of the binary. The following list shows example URLs for platform binaries compatible with Linux AMD64:

- kubectl: *https://dl.k8s.io/v1.26.1/bin/linux/amd64/kubectl.sha256*
- kubeadm: *https://dl.k8s.io/v1.26.1/bin/linux/amd64/kubeadm.sha256*
- kubelet: *https://dl.k8s.io/v1.26.1/bin/linux/amd64/kubelet.sha256*
- kube-apiserver: *https://dl.k8s.io/v1.26.1/bin/linux/amd64/kube-apiserver.sha256*

You'll have to use an operating system-specific hash code validation tool to check the validity of a binary. You may have to install the tool if you do not have it available on your machine yet. The following commands show the usage of the tool for different operating systems, as explained in the Kubernetes documentation (*https://oreil.ly/2FmVm*):

- Linux: `echo "$(cat kubectl.sha256) kubectl" | sha256sum --check`
- MacOSX: `echo "$(cat kubectl.sha256) kubectl" | shasum -a 256 --check`
- Windows with Powershell: `$($(CertUtil -hashfile .\kubectl.exe SHA256) [1] -replace " ", "") -eq $(type .\kubectl.exe.sha256)`

The following commands demonstrate downloading the kubeadm binary for version 1.26.1 and its corresponding SHA256 hash file:

```
$ curl -LO "https://dl.k8s.io/v1.26.1/bin/linux/amd64/kubeadm"
$ curl -LO "https://dl.k8s.io/v1.26.1/bin/linux/amd64/kubeadm.sha256"
```

The validation tool shasum can verify if the checksum matches:

```
$ echo "$(cat kubeadm.sha256)  kubeadm" | shasum -a 256 --check
kubeadm: OK
```

The previous command returned with an "OK" message. The binary file wasn't tampered with. Any other message indicates a potential security risk when executing the binary.

Summary

The domain "cluster setup" dials in on security aspects relevant to setting up a Kubernetes cluster. Even though you might be creating a cluster from scratch with kubeadm, that doesn't mean you are necessarily following best practices. Using kube-bench to detect potential security risks is a good start. Fix the issues reported on by the tool one by one. You may also want to check client and server binaries against their checksums to ensure that they haven't been modified by an attacker. Some organizations use a Dashboard to manage the cluster and its objects. Ensure that authentication and authorization for the Dashboard restrict access to a small subset of stakeholders.

An important security aspect is network communication. Pod-to-Pod communication is unrestricted by default. Have a close look at your application architecture running inside of Kubernetes. Only allow directional network traffic from and to Pods to fulfill the requirements of your architecture. Deny all other network traffic. When exposing the application outside of the cluster, make sure that Ingress objects have been configured with TLS termination. This will ensure that the data is encrypted both ways so that attackers cannot observe sensitive information like passwords sent between a client and the Kubernetes cluster.

Exam Essentials

Understand the purpose and effects of network policies
> By default, Pod-to-Pod communication is unrestricted. Instantiate a default deny rule to restrict Pod-to-Pod network traffic with the principle of least privilege. The attribute `spec.podSelector` of a network policy selects the target Pod the rules apply to based on label selection. The ingress and egress rules define Pods, namespaces, IP addresses, and ports for allowing incoming and outgoing traffic. Network policies can be aggregated. A default deny rule may disallow ingress and/or egress traffic. An additional network policy can open up those rules with a more fine-grained definition.

Practice the use of kube-bench to detect cluster component vulnerabilities
> The Kubernetes CIS Benchmark is a set of best practices for recommended security settings in a production Kubernetes environment. You can automate the process of detecting security risks with the help of the tool kube-bench. The generated report from running kube-bench describes detailed remediation actions to fix a detected issue. Learn how to interpret the results and how to mitigate the issue.

Know how to configure Ingress with TLS termination
> An Ingress can be configured to send and receive encrypted data by exposing an HTTPS endpoint. For this to work, you need to create a TLS Secret object and assign it a TLS certificate and key. The Secret can then be consumed by the Ingress using the attribute `spec.tls[]`.

Know how to configure GUI elements for secure access
> GUI elements, such as the Kubernetes Dashboard, provide a convenient way to manage objects. Attackers can cause harm to your cluster if the application isn't protected from unauthorized access. For the exam, you need to know how to properly set up RBAC for specific stakeholders. Moreover, you are expected to have a rough understanding of security-related command line arguments. Practice the installation process for the Dashboard, learn how to tweak its command line arguments, and understand the effects of setting permissions for different users.

Know how to detect modified platform binaries

Platform binaries like kubectl and kubeadm can be verified against their corresponding hash code. Know where to find the hash file and how to use a validation tool to identify if the binary has been tempered with.

Sample Exercises

Solutions to these exercises are available in the Appendix.

1. Create a network policy that denies egress traffic to any domain outside of the cluster. The network policy applies to Pods with the label app=backend and also allows egress traffic for port 53 for UDP and TCP to Pods in any other namespace.

2. Create a Pod named allowed that runs the busybox:1.36.0 image on port 80 and assign it the label app=frontend. Make a curl call to http://google.com. The network call should be allowed, as the network policy doesn't apply to the Pod.

3. Create another Pod named denied that runs the busybox:1.36.0 image on port 80 and assign it the label app=backend. Make a curl call to http://google.com. The network call should be blocked.

4. Install the Kubernetes Dashboard or make sure that it is already installed. In the namespace kubernetes-dashboard, create a ServiceAccount named observer-user. Moreover, create the corresponding ClusterRole and ClusterRoleBinding. The ServiceAccount should only be allowed to view Deployments. All other operations should be denied. As an example, create the Deployment named deploy in the default namespace with the following command: kubectl create deployment deploy --image=nginx --replicas=3.

5. Create a token for the ServiceAccount named observer-user that will never expire. Log into the Dashboard using the token. Ensure that only Deployments can be viewed and not any other type of resource.

6. Download the binary file of the API server with version 1.26.1 on Linux AMD64. Download the SH256 checksum file for the API-server executable of version 1.23.1. Run the OS-specific verification tool and observe the result.

CHAPTER 3
Cluster Hardening

The domain "cluster hardening" touches on topics important to keep a cluster as secure as possible once it has been set up and configured initially. As part of the discussion of this chapter, you may notice that I will reference concepts and practices that usually fall into the hands of Kubernetes administrators. Where appropriate, I will provide links to the topics that have already been covered by the CKA exam.

At a high level, this chapter covers the following concepts:

- Restricting access to the Kubernetes API
- Configuring role-based access control (RBAC) to minimize exposure
- Exercising caution in using service accounts
- Updating Kubernetes frequently

Interacting with the Kubernetes API

The API server is the gateway to the Kubernetes cluster. Any human user, client (e.g., kubectl), cluster component, or service account will access the API server by making a RESTful API call via HTTPS. It is *the* central point for performing operations like creating a Pod, or deleting a Service.

In this section, we'll only focus on the security-specific aspects relevant to the API server. For a detailed discussion on the inner workings of the API server and the usage of the Kubernetes API, refer to the book *Managing Kubernetes* by Brendan Burns and Craig Tracey (O'Reilly).

Processing a Request

Figure 3-1 illustrates the stages a request goes through when a call is made to the API server. For reference, you can find more information in the Kubernetes documentation (*https://oreil.ly/DuLdf*).

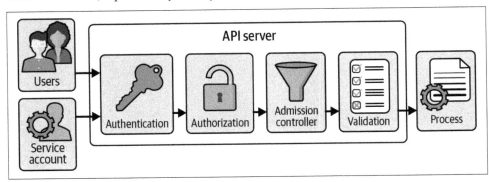

Figure 3-1. API server request processing

The first stage of request processing is *authentication*. Authentication validates the identity of the caller by inspecting the client certificates or bearer tokens. If the bearer token is associated with a service account, then it will be verified here.

The second stage determines if the identity provided in the first stage can access the verb and HTTP path request. Therefore, stage two deals with *authorization* of the request, which is implemented with the standard Kubernetes RBAC model. Here, we'd ensure that the service account is allowed to list Pods or create a new Service object if that's what has been requested.

The third stage of request processing deals with *admission control*. Admission control verifies if the request is well-formed and potentially needs to be modified before the request is processed. An admission control policy could, for example, ensure that the request for creating a Pod includes the definition of a specific label. If it doesn't define the label, then the request is rejected.

The last stage of the process ensures that the resource included in the request is valid. Request *validation* can be implemented as part of admission control but doesn't have to be. For example, this stage ensures that the name of a Service object sticks to the standard Kubernetes naming rules for provided DNS names.

Connecting to the API Server

It's easy to determine the endpoint for the API server by running the following:

```
$ kubectl cluster-info
Kubernetes control plane is running at https://172.28.40.5:6443
...
```

For the given Kubernetes cluster, the API server has been exposed via the URL *https://172.28.40.5:6443*. Alternatively, you can also have a look at the command line options `--advertise-address` and `--secure-port` in the configuration file of the API server to determine the endpoint. You can find the API server configuration file at `/etc/kubernetes/manifests/kube-apiserver.yaml`.

Configuring an insecure port for the API server

The ability to configure the API server to use an insecure port (e.g., 80) has been deprecated in Kubernetes 1.10. With version 1.24, the insecure port flags `--port` and `--insecure-port` have been removed completely and therefore cannot be used to configure the API server anymore. See the release notes (*https://oreil.ly/OTsmV*) for more information.

Using the kubernetes Service

Kubernetes makes accessing the API server a little bit more convenient for specific use cases. For example, you may want to send a request to the Kubernetes API from a Pod. Instead of using the IP address and port for the API server, you can simply refer to the Service named `kubernetes.default.svc` instead. This special Service lives in the `default` namespace and is stood up by the cluster automatically. Deleting the Service will automatically recreate it. You can easily find the Service with the following command:

```
$ kubectl get service kubernetes
NAME        TYPE       CLUSTER-IP   EXTERNAL-IP   PORT(S)   AGE
kubernetes  ClusterIP  10.96.0.1    <none>        443/TCP   32s
```

Upon inspection of the endpoints of this Service, you will see that it points to the IP address and port of the API server, as demonstrated by executing the following command:

```
$ kubectl get endpoints kubernetes
NAME        ENDPOINTS          AGE
kubernetes  172.28.40.5:6443   4m3s
```

The IP address and port of the Service is also exposed to the Pod via environment variables. You can read the values of the environment variables from a program running inside of a container. The Service's IP address is reflected by the environment variable `KUBERNETES_SERVICE_HOST`. The port can be accessed using the environment variable `KUBERNETES_SERVICE_PORT`. To render the environment, simply access the environment variables using the `env` command in a temporary Pod:

```
$ kubectl run kubernetes-envs --image=alpine:3.16.2 -it --rm --restart=Never \
  -- env
KUBERNETES_SERVICE_HOST=10.96.0.1
KUBERNETES_SERVICE_PORT=443
```

We will use the `kubernetes` Service in the section "Minimizing Permissions for a Service Account" on page 53.

Anonymous access

The following command makes an anonymous call to the API using the `curl` command line tool to list all namespaces. The option `-k` avoids verifying the server's TLS certificate:

```
$ curl https://172.28.40.5:6443/api/v1/namespaces -k
{
  "kind": "Status",
  "apiVersion": "v1",
  "metadata": {},
  "status": "Failure",
  "message": "namespaces is forbidden: User \"system:anonymous\" cannot list \
            resource \"namespaces\" in API group \"\" at the cluster scope",
  "reason": "Forbidden",
  "details": {
    "kind": "namespaces"
  },
  "code": 403
}
```

As you can see from the JSON-formatted HTTP response body, anonymous calls are accepted by the API server but do not have the appropriate permissions for the operation. Internally, Kubernetes maps the call to the username `system:anonymous` (*https://oreil.ly/_HrbF*), which effectively isn't authorized to execute the operation.

Access with a client certificate

To make a request as an authorized user, you need to either create a new one or use the existing, default user with administrator permissions named kubernetes-admin. We won't go through the process of creating a new user right now. For more information on creating a user, refer to "Restricting User Permissions" on page 48.

The following command lists all available users, including their client certificate and key:

```
$ kubectl config view --raw
apiVersion: v1
clusters:
- cluster:
    certificate-authority-data: LS0tLS1CRUdJTiBDRVJUSUZJQ0FURS0tL...  ❶
    server: https://172.28.132.5:6443
  name: kubernetes
contexts:
- context:
    cluster: kubernetes
    user: kubernetes-admin
```

```
     name: kubernetes-admin@kubernetes
current-context: kubernetes-admin@kubernetes
kind: Config
preferences: {}
users:
- name: kubernetes-admin ❷
  user:
    client-certificate-data: LS0tLS1CRUdJTiBDRVJUSUZJQ0FURS0tL... ❸
    client-key-data: LS0tLS1CRUdJTiBSU0EgUFJJVkFURSBLRVktL... ❹
```

❶ The base64-encoded value of the certificate authority

❷ The user entry with administrator permissions created by default

❸ The base64-encoded value of the user's client certificate

❹ The base64-encoded value of the user's private key

For making a call using the user kubernetes-admin, we'll need to extract the base64-encoded values for the CA, client certificate, and private key into files as a base64-decoded value. The following command copies the base64-encoded value and uses the tool base64 to decode it before it is written to a file. The CA value will be stored in the file ca, the client certificate value in kubernetes-admin.crt, and the private key in kubernetes-admin.key:

```
$ echo LS0tLS1CRUdJTiBDRVJUSUZJQ0FURS0tL... | base64 -d > ca
$ echo LS0tLS1CRUdJTiBDRVJUSUZJQ0FURS0tL... | base64 -d > kubernetes-admin.crt
$ echo LS0tLS1CRUdJTiBSU0EgUFJJVkFURSBLRVktL... | base64 - \
> kubernetes-admin.key
```

You can now point the curl command to those files with the relevant command line option. The request to the API server should properly authenticate and return all existing namespaces, as the kubernetes-admin has the appropriated permissions:

```
$ curl --cacert ca --cert kubernetes-admin.crt --key kubernetes-admin.key \
  https://172.28.132.5:6443/api/v1/namespaces
{
  "kind": "NamespaceList",
  "apiVersion": "v1",
  "metadata": {
    "resourceVersion": "2387"
  },
  "items": [
    ...
  ]
}
```

Restricting Access to the API Server

If you're exposing the API server to the internet, ask yourself if it is necessary. Some cloud providers offer the option of creating a private cluster, which will limit or completely disable public access to the API server. For more information, see the documentation pages for EKS (*https://oreil.ly/W4Oma*) and GKE (*https://oreil.ly/c7G-g*).

If you are operating an on-premises Kubernetes cluster, you will need to instantiate firewall rules that prevent access to the API server. Setting up firewall rules is out of scope for the exam and therefore won't be discussed in this book.

Scenario: An Attacker Can Call the API Server from the Internet

Cloud providers sometimes expose the API server to the internet to simplify administrative access. An attacker can try to make an anonymous request to the API server endpoint by declining to provide a client certificate or bearer token. If the attacker is lucky enough to capture user credentials, then an authenticated call can be performed. Depending on the permissions assigned to the user, malicious operations can be executed. Figure 3-2 illustrates an attacker calling the API server from the internet.

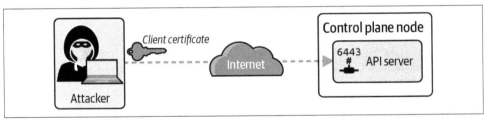

Figure 3-2. An attacker calls the API server from the internet

In this chapter, we will have a look at how to restrict access to the API server and how to implement RBAC with limited permissions by example. "Understanding Open Policy Agent (OPA) and Gatekeeper" on page 95 will review admission control with the help of OPA Gateway.

Restricting User Permissions

We've seen that we can use the credentials of the kubernetes-admin user to make calls to the Kubernetes API. This user should be used very sparingly, nor should the credentials be shared with a lot of humans. A lot of damage can be done if the credentials fall into the wrong hands. Reserve this user exclusively for humans in charge of cluster administration.

For other stakeholders of your Kubernetes cluster, you should set up a dedicated user with a limited set of permissions. You may have specific roles in your organization you can map to. For example, you may have a developer role that should be allowed to manage Deployments, Pods, ConfigMaps, Secrets, and Services, but nothing else. To create a new user and assign the relevant RBAC permissions, refer to the Kubernetes documentation (*https://oreil.ly/n8EMD*). In a nutshell, there are four steps:

1. Create a private key.
2. Create and approve a CertificateSigningRequest.
3. Create a Role and a RoleBinding.
4. Add the user to the kubeconfig file (*https://oreil.ly/OKs9g*).

We will cover the process in detail, but will come back to the RBAC concept in more detail for a service account in "Minimizing Permissions for a Service Account" on page 53.

Creating a private key

Create a private key using the openssl executable. Provide an expressive file name, such as <username>.key:

```
$ openssl genrsa -out johndoe.key 2048
Generating RSA private key, 2048 bit long modulus
...+
.................................................................+
e is 65537 (0x10001)
```

Create a certificate signing request (CSR) in a file with the extension .csr. You need to provide the private key from the previous step. The following command uses the username johndoe when asked for entering the "Common Name" value. All other input requests are optional and can be filled in as needed:

```
$ openssl req -new -key johndoe.key -out johndoe.csr
You are about to be asked to enter information that will be incorporated
into your certificate request.
What you are about to enter is what is called a Distinguished Name or a DN.
There are quite a few fields but you can leave some blank
For some fields there will be a default value,
If you enter '.', the field will be left blank.
-----
Country Name (2 letter code) []:
State or Province Name (full name) []:
Locality Name (eg, city) []:
Organization Name (eg, company) []:
Organizational Unit Name (eg, section) []:
Common Name (eg, fully qualified host name) []:johndoe
Email Address []:
```

```
Please enter the following 'extra' attributes
to be sent with your certificate request
A challenge password []:
```

Retrieve the base64-encoded value of the CSR file content with the following command. You will need it when creating the CertificateSigningRequest object in the next step:

```
$ cat johndoe.csr | base64 | tr -d "\n"
LS0tLS1CRUdJTiBDRVJUSUZJQ0FURSBSRVFVRVNULS0tL...
```

Creating and approving a CertificateSigningRequest

The following script creates a CertificateSigningRequest object. A CertificateSigning-Request resource (*https://oreil.ly/ltFbE*) is used to request that a certificate be signed by a denoted signer:

```
$ cat <<EOF | kubectl apply -f -
apiVersion: certificates.k8s.io/v1
kind: CertificateSigningRequest
metadata:
  name: johndoe
spec:
  request: LS0tLS1CRUdJTiBDRVJUSUZJQ0FURSBSRVFVRVNULS0tL...
  signerName: kubernetes.io/kube-apiserver-client
  expirationSeconds: 86400
  usages:
  - client auth
EOF
certificatesigningrequest.certificates.k8s.io/johndoe created
```

The value for kubernetes.io/kube-apiserver-client for the attribute spec.signer Name signs certificates that will be honored as client certificates by the API server. Use the base64-encoded value from the previous step and assign it as a value to the attribute spec.request. Finally, the optional attribute spec.expirationSeconds determines the lifespan of the certificate. The assigned value 86400 makes the certificate valid for a one day. You will want to increase the expiration time depending on how long you want the certificate to last, or simply refrain from adding the attribute.

After creating the CertificateSigningRequest object, the condition will be "Pending." You will need to approve the signing request within 24 hours or the object will be deleted automatically as a means to garbage-collect unnecessary objects in the cluster:

```
$ kubectl get csr johndoe
NAME        AGE    SIGNERNAME                             REQUESTOR      \
  REQUESTEDDURATION    CONDITION
johndoe     6s     kubernetes.io/kube-apiserver-client    minikube-user \
  24h                  Pending
```

Use the certificate approve command to approve the signing request. As a result, the condition changes to "Approved,Issued":

```
$ kubectl certificate approve johndoe
certificatesigningrequest.certificates.k8s.io/johndoe approved
$ kubectl get csr johndoe
NAME        AGE    SIGNERNAME                          REQUESTOR       \
  REQUESTEDDURATION    CONDITION
johndoe     17s    kubernetes.io/kube-apiserver-client  minikube-user \
  24h                  Approved,Issued
```

Finally, export the issued certificate from the approved CertificateSigningRequest object:

```
$ kubectl get csr johndoe -o jsonpath={.status.certificate}| base64 \
  -d > johndoe.crt
```

Creating a Role and a RoleBinding

It's time to assign RBAC permissions. In this step, you will create a Role and a RoleBinding for the user. The Role models an "application developer" role within the organization. A developer should only be allowed to get, list, update, and delete Pods. The following imperative command creates the Role object:

```
$ kubectl create role developer --verb=create --verb=get --verb=list \
  --verb=update --verb=delete --resource=pods
role.rbac.authorization.k8s.io/developer created
```

Next, we'll bind the Role to the user named johndoe. Use the imperative command create rolebinding to achieve that:

```
$ kubectl create rolebinding developer-binding-johndoe --role=developer \
  --user=johndoe
rolebinding.rbac.authorization.k8s.io/developer-binding-johndoe created
```

Adding the user to the kubeconfig file

In this last step, you will need to add the user to the kubeconfig file and create the context for a user. Be aware that the cluster name is minikube in the following command, as we are trying this out in a minikube installation:

```
$ kubectl config set-credentials johndoe --client-key=johndoe.key \
  --client-certificate=johndoe.crt --embed-certs=true
User "johndoe" set.
$ kubectl config set-context johndoe --cluster=minikube --user=johndoe
Context "johndoe" created.
```

Verifying the permissions

It's time to switch to the user context named johndoe:

```
$ kubectl config use-context johndoe
Switched to context "johndoe".
```

Using kubectl as the client that makes calls to the API server, we'll verify that the operation should be allowed. The API call for listing all Pods in the default namespace was authenticated and authorized:

```
$ kubectl get pods
No resources found in default namespace.
```

The output of the command indicates that the default namespace doesn't contain any Pod object at this time but the call was successful. Let's also test the negative case. Listing namespaces is a non-permitted operation for the user. Executing the relevant kubectl command will return with an error message:

```
$ kubectl get namespaces
Error from server (Forbidden): namespaces is forbidden: User "johndoe" cannot \
list resource "namespaces" in API group "" at the cluster scope
```

Once you are done with verifying permissions, you may want to switch back to the context with admin permissions:

```
$ kubectl config use-context minikube
Switched to context "minikube".
```

Scenario: An Attacker Can Call the API Server from a Service Account

A user represents a real person who commonly interacts with the Kubernetes cluster using the kubectl executable or the UI dashboard. Under rare conditions, applications running inside of a Pod's container need to interact with the Kubernetes API. A typical example for such a requirement is the package manager Helm (*https:// helm.sh*). Helm manages Kubernetes resources based on the YAML manifests bundled in a Helm chart. Kubernetes uses a service account to authenticate the Helm service process with the API server through an authentication token. This service account can be assigned to a Pod and mapped to RBAC rules.

An attacker who gains access to the Pod will likely also be able to misuse the service account to make calls to the Kubernetes API, as shown in Figure 3-3.

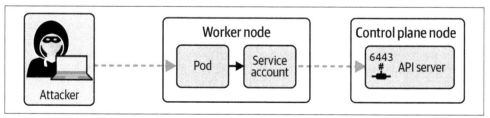

Figure 3-3. An attacker uses a service account to call the API server

Minimizing Permissions for a Service Account

It's important to limit the permissions to only those service accounts that are really necessary for the application to function. The next sections will explain how to achieve this to minimize the potential attack surface.

For this scenario to work, you'll need to create a ServiceAccount object and assign it to the Pod. Service accounts can be tied in with RBAC and assigned a Role and RoleBinding to define what operations they should be allowed to perform.

Binding the service account to a Pod

As a starting point, we are going to a set up a Pod that lists all Pods and Deployments in the namespace k97 by calling the Kubernetes API. The call is made as part of an infinite loop every ten seconds. The response from the API call will be written to standard output accessible via the Pod's logs.

To authenticate against the API server, we'll send a bearer token associated with the service account used by the Pod. The default behavior of a service account is to auto-mount API credentials on the path /var/run/secrets/kubernetes.io/service account/token. We'll simply get the contents of the file using the cat command line tool and send them along as a header for the HTTP request. Example 3-1 defines the namespace, the service account, and the Pod in a single YAML manifest file setup.yaml.

Example 3-1. YAML manifest for assigning a service account to a Pod

```
apiVersion: v1
kind: Namespace
metadata:
  name: k97
---
apiVersion: v1
kind: ServiceAccount
metadata:
  name: sa-api
  namespace: k97
---
apiVersion: v1
kind: Pod
metadata:
  name: list-objects
  namespace: k97
spec:
  serviceAccountName: sa-api
  containers:
  - name: pods
    image: alpine/curl:3.14
```

```
          command: ['sh', '-c', 'while true; do curl -s -k -m 5 -H \
                  "Authorization: Bearer $(cat /var/run/secrets/kubernetes.io/ \
                  serviceaccount/token)" https://kubernetes.default.svc.cluster. \
                  local/api/v1/namespaces/k97/pods; sleep 10; done']
      - name: deployments
        image: alpine/curl:3.14
        command: ['sh', '-c', 'while true; do curl -s -k -m 5 -H \
                  "Authorization: Bearer $(cat /var/run/secrets/kubernetes.io/ \
                  serviceaccount/token)" https://kubernetes.default.svc.cluster. \
                  local/apis/apps/v1/namespaces/k97/deployments; sleep 10; done']
```

Create the objects from the YAML file with the following command:

```
$ kubectl apply -f setup.yaml
namespace/k97 created
serviceaccount/sa-api created
pod/list-objects created
```

Verifying the default permissions

The Pod named list-objects makes a call to the API server to retrieve the list of Pods and Deployments in dedicated containers. The container pods performs the call to list Pods. The container deployments sends a request to the API server to list Deployments.

As explained in the Kubernetes documentation (*https://oreil.ly/gBp30*), the default RBAC policies do not grant any permissions to service accounts outside of the kube-system namespace. The logs of the containers pods and deployments return an error message indicating that the service account sa-api is not authorized to list the resources:

```
$ kubectl logs list-objects -c pods -n k97
{
  "kind": "Status",
  "apiVersion": "v1",
  "metadata": {},
  "status": "Failure",
  "message": "pods is forbidden: User \"system:serviceaccount:k97:sa-api\" \
              cannot list resource \"pods\" in API group \"\" in the \
              namespace \"k97\"",
  "reason": "Forbidden",
  "details": {
    "kind": "pods"
  },
  "code": 403
}
$ kubectl logs list-objects -c deployments -n k97
{
  "kind": "Status",
  "apiVersion": "v1",
  "metadata": {},
```

```
  "status": "Failure",
  "message": "deployments.apps is forbidden: User \
              \"system:serviceaccount:k97:sa-api\" cannot list resource \
              \"deployments\" in API group \"apps\" in the namespace \
              \"k97\"",
  "reason": "Forbidden",
  "details": {
    "group": "apps",
    "kind": "deployments"
  },
  "code": 403
}
```

Next up, we'll stand up a ClusterRole and RoleBinding object with the required API permissions to perform the necessary calls.

Creating the ClusterRole

Start by defining the ClusterRole named `list-pods-clusterrole` shown in Example 3-2 in the file `clusterrole.yaml`. The set of the rules only adds the Pod resource and the verb `list`.

Example 3-2. YAML manifest for a ClusterRole that allows listing Pods

```
apiVersion: rbac.authorization.k8s.io/v1
kind: ClusterRole
metadata:
  name: list-pods-clusterrole
rules:
- apiGroups: [""]
  resources: ["pods"]
  verbs: ["list"]
```

Create the object by pointing to its corresponding YAML manifest file:

```
$ kubectl apply -f clusterrole.yaml
clusterrole.rbac.authorization.k8s.io/list-pods-clusterrole created
```

Creating the RoleBinding

Example 3-3 defines the YAML manifest for the RoleBinding in the file `rolebind ing.yaml`. The RoleBinding maps the ClusterRole `list-pods-clusterrole` to the service account named `sa-pod-api` and only applies to the namespace `k97`.

Example 3-3. YAML manifest for a RoleBinding attached to a service account

```
apiVersion: rbac.authorization.k8s.io/v1
kind: RoleBinding
metadata:
  name: serviceaccount-pod-rolebinding
```

```
  namespace: k97
subjects:
- kind: ServiceAccount
  name: sa-api
roleRef:
  kind: ClusterRole
  name: list-pods-clusterrole
  apiGroup: rbac.authorization.k8s.io
```

Create both the RoleBinding object using the `apply` command:

```
$ kubectl apply -f rolebinding.yaml
rolebinding.rbac.authorization.k8s.io/serviceaccount-pod-rolebinding created
```

Verifying the granted permissions

With the granted `list` permissions, the service account can now properly retrieve all the Pods in the k97 namespace. The `curl` command in the pods container succeeds, as shown in the following output:

```
$ kubectl logs list-objects -c pods -n k97
{
  "kind": "PodList",
  "apiVersion": "v1",
  "metadata": {
    "resourceVersion": "628"
  },
  "items": [
      {
        "metadata": {
          "name": "list-objects",
          "namespace": "k97",
          ...
      }
  ]
}
```

We did not grant any permissions to the service account for other resources. Listing the Deployments in the k97 namespace still fails. The following output shows the response from the `curl` command in the `deployments` namespace:

```
$ kubectl logs list-objects -c deployments -n k97
{
  "kind": "Status",
  "apiVersion": "v1",
  "metadata": {},
  "status": "Failure",
  "message": "deployments.apps is forbidden: User \
              \"system:serviceaccount:k97:sa-api\" cannot list resource \
              \"deployments\" in API group \"apps\" in the namespace \
              \"k97\"",
  "reason": "Forbidden",
```

```
    "details": {
      "group": "apps",
      "kind": "deployments"
    },
    "code": 403
  }
```

Feel free to modify the ClusterRole object to allow listing Deployment objects as well.

Disabling automounting of a service account token

The Pod described in the previous section used the service account's token as a means to authenticate against the API server. Mounting the token file at /var/run/secrets/kubernetes.io/serviceaccount/token is the standard behavior of every service account. You will really only need the contents of the file if the Pod actually interacts with the Kubernetes API. In all other cases, this behavior poses a potential security risk as access to the Pod will directly lead an attacker to the token.

You can disable the automount behavior for a service account object by assigning the value false to the attribute automountServiceAccountToken, as shown in Example 3-4.

Example 3-4. Opting out of a service account's token automount behavior

```
apiVersion: v1
kind: ServiceAccount
metadata:
  name: sa-api
  namespace: k97
automountServiceAccountToken: false
```

If you want to disable the automount behavior for individual Pods, use the attribute spec.automountServiceAccountToken in the Pod definition. Example 3-5 shows a YAML manifest for a Pod.

Example 3-5. Disabling token automounting for a service account in a Pod

```
apiVersion: v1
kind: Pod
metadata:
  name: list-objects
  namespace: k97
spec:
  serviceAccountName: sa-api
  automountServiceAccountToken: false
  ...
```

Generating a service account token

There are a variety of use cases that speak for wanting to create a service account that *disables* token automounting. For example, you may need access to the Kubernetes API from an external tool or a continuous delivery pipeline to query for information about existing objects. Authenticating against the API server in those scenarios still requires a token. The scenarios listed do not necessarily run a Pod with an assigned service account, but simply perform a RESTful API call from a tool like `curl`.

To create a token manually, execute the `create token` command and provide the name of the service account as an argument. The output of the command renders the token:

```
$ kubectl create token sa-api
eyJhbGciOiJSUzI1NiIsImtpZCI6IjBtQkJzVWlsQjl...
```

You'll need to store the token in a safe place, e.g., a password manager. You cannot retrieve the token again if you lose it. You can only recreate it with the same command, which will automatically invalidate the previous token. All references that use the token will have to be changed.

For automated processes, it might be helpful to generate a token with a limited lifespan. The `--duration` will automatically invalidate the token after the "time-to-life" runs out:

```
$ kubectl create token sa-api --duration 10m
eyJhbGciOiJSUzI1NiIsImtpZCI6IjBtQkJzVWlsQjl...
```

Creating a Secret for a service account

With Kubernetes 1.24, a ServiceAccount object does not automatically create a corresponding Secret object containing the token anymore. See the release notes (*https://oreil.ly/MSPuX*) for more information. Listing the ServiceAccount object renders 0 for the number of Secrets. The object also doesn't contain the `secrets` attribute anymore in the YAML representation:

```
$ kubectl get serviceaccount sa-api -n k97
NAME     SECRETS   AGE
sa-api   0         42m
```

You can either generate the token using the `create token` command, as described in "Generating a service account token" on page 58, or manually create a corresponding Secret. Example 3-6 shows a YAML manifest for such a Secret.

Example 3-6. Creating a Secret for a service account manually

```
apiVersion: v1
kind: Secret
metadata:
```

```
  name: sa-api-secret
  namespace: k97
  annotations:
    kubernetes.io/service-account.name: sa-api
type: kubernetes.io/service-account-token
```

To assign the service account to the Secret, add the annotation with the key kuber
netes.io/service-account.name. The following command creates the Secret object:

```
$ kubectl create -f secret.yaml
secret/sa-api-secret created
```

You can find the token in the "Data" section when describing the Secret object:

```
$ kubectl describe secret sa-api-secret -n k97
...
Data
====
ca.crt:     1111 bytes
namespace:  3 bytes
token:      eyJhbGciOiJSUzI1NiIsImtpZCI6IjBtQkJzVWlsQjl...
```

Updating Kubernetes Frequently

Installing a Kubernetes cluster with a specific version is not a one-time fire-and-
forget operation. Even if you used the latest Long-Term Support (LTS) Release at
the time of installation, it does not guarantee that your cluster is without security
vulnerabilities.

As time goes by, security-related bugs and weaknesses will be discovered. This state-
ment includes the underlying operating system and the dependencies the cluster
nodes run on. An attacker can easily look up security vulnerabilities in the publicly
disclosed Common Vulnerabilities and Exposures (CVE) database (*https://oreil.ly/
FHhXD*) and exploit them.

Versioning Scheme

It's up to the cluster administrator to update the Kubernetes version across all
nodes on a regular basis. Kubernetes follows the semantic versioning scheme (*https://
semver.org*). A Semantic Version consists of a major version, minor version, and patch
version. For example, for the Kubernetes version 1.24.3, the major version is 1, the
minor version is 24, and the patch version is 3.

Each portion of the version carries a specific meaning. A change to the major version
portion indicates a breaking change. Incrementing the minor version portion means
that new functionality has been added in a backward-compatible manner. The patch
version portion simply fixes a bug.

Breaking changes in Kubernetes with minor version updates

It's important to mention that Kubernetes doesn't always stick to the strict interpretation of semantic versioning. For example, the PodSecurityPolicy (PSP) admission controller has been replaced by the Pod Security Admission concept in version 1.25.0 (*https://oreil.ly/JE-i8*). Conventionally, those changes should only happen with a major version update. Reference the Kubernetes deprecation policy (*https://oreil.ly/on9lu*) for a better understanding on how an API, a flag, or a feature is phased out.

Release Cadence

You can expect a new minor version release (*https://oreil.ly/LGIn5*) of Kubernetes every three months. The release may include new features and additional bug fixes. Security fixes may be implemented as needed for the latest release of Kubernetes and will be backported to the two minor releases before that. Always staying on top of updating to the latest releases for your own cluster(s) takes quite a bit of people-power. You will need to reserve time for those activities accordingly.

Performing the Upgrade Process

It is recommended to upgrade from a minor version to the next higher one (e.g., from 1.23 to 1.24), or from a patch version to a more recent one (e.g., from 1.24.1 to 1.24.3). Abstain from jumping up multiple minor versions to avoid unexpected side effects.

You can find a full description of the upgrade steps (*https://oreil.ly/RxC9j*) in the official Kubernetes documentation. Figure 3-4 illustrates the upgrade process on a high level.

The cluster version upgrade process is already part of the CKA exam. Given that you have to pass the CKA as a prerequisite, I would assume that you already know how to perform the process. For a detailed description, refer to *Certified Kubernetes Administrator (CKA) Study Guide*.

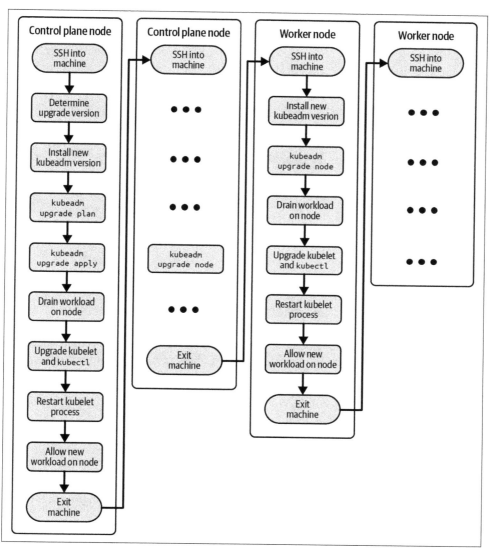

Figure 3-4. Process for a cluster version upgrade

Summary

Users, clients applications (such as `kubectl` or `curl`), Pods using service accounts, and cluster components all communicate with the API server to manage objects. It's paramount to secure the API server to prevent access with malicious intent.

To minimize the attack surface area, avoid exposing the API server to the internet using firewall rules. For every user or service account, restrict the permissions to execute operations against the Kubernetes API to the bare minimum using RBAC rules. With minimized permissions, attackers can cause far less damage in case they can gain access to credentials.

Make sure to upgrade the version of your Kubernetes cluster. Incorporating bug and security fixes will decrease the risk of exposing unnecessary vulnerabilities attackers can use to their advantage.

Exam Essentials

Practice interacting with the Kubernetes API.
  This chapter demonstrated the different ways to communicate with the Kubernetes API. We performed API requests by switching to a user context, and with the help of a RESTful API call using `curl`. You will need to understand how to determine the endpoint of the API server and how to use different authentication methods, e.g., client credentials and bearer tokens. Explore the Kubernetes API and its endpoints on your own for broader exposure.

Understand the implications of defining RBAC rules for users and service accounts.
  Anonymous user requests to the Kubernetes API will not allow any substantial operations. For requests coming from a user or a service account, you will need to carefully analyze permissions granted to the subject. Learn the ins and outs of defining RBAC rules by creating the relevant objects to control permissions. Service accounts automount a token when used in a Pod. Only expose the token as a Volume if you are intending to make API calls from the Pod.

Be aware of Kubernetes release cadence and the need for upgrading the cluster.
  A Kubernetes cluster needs to be cared for over time for security reasons. Attackers may try to take advantage of known vulnerabilities in outdated Kubernetes versions. The version upgrade process is part of every administrator's job and shouldn't be ignored.

Sample Exercises

Solutions to these exercises are available in the Appendix.

1. Create a client certificate and key for the user named jill in the group observer. With the admin context, create the context for the user jill.

2. For the group (not the user!), define a Role and RoleBinding in the default namespace that allow the verbs get, list, and watch for the resources Pods, ConfigMaps, and Secrets. Create the objects.

3. Switch to the user context and execute a kubectl command that allows one of the granted operations, and one kubectl command that should not be permitted. Switch back to the admin context.

4. Create a Pod named service-list in the namespace t23. The container uses the image alpine/curl:3.14 and makes a curl call to the Kubernetes API that lists Service objects in the default namespace in an infinite loop. Create and attach the service account api-call. Inspect the container logs after the Pod has been started. What response do you expect to see from the curl command?

5. Assign a ClusterRole and RoleBinding to the service account that only allows the operation needed by the Pod. Have a look at the response from the curl command.

6. Configure the Pod so that automounting of the service account token is disabled. Retrieve the token value and use it directly with the curl command. Make sure that the curl command can still authorize the operation.

7. Navigate to the directory *app-a/ch03/upgrade-version* of the checked-out GitHub repository *bmuschko/cks-study-guide* (*https://oreil.ly/sImXZ*). Start up the VMs running the cluster using the command vagrant up. Upgrade all nodes of the cluster from Kubernetes 1.25.6 to 1.26.1. The cluster consists of a single control plane node named kube-control-plane, and one worker node named kube-worker-1. Once done, shut down the cluster using vagrant destroy -f.

   Prerequisite: This exercise requires the installation of the tools Vagrant (*https://oreil.ly/FiyeH*) and VirtualBox (*https://oreil.ly/WW8IK*).

CHAPTER 4

System Hardening

The domain "system hardening" deals with security aspects relevant to the underlying host system running the Kubernetes cluster nodes. Topics discussed here touch on techniques and configuration options that are fundamentally Linux core functionality. This includes disabling services and removing packages, managing users and groups, disabling ports, and setting up firewall rules. Finally, this chapter discusses Linux kernel hardening tools that can restrict what operations a process running in a container can perform on a host level.

At a high level, this chapter covers the following concepts:

- Minimizing the host OS footprint
- Minimizing IAM roles
- Minimizing external access to the network
- Using kernel hardening tools like AppArmor and seccomp

Minimizing the Host OS Footprint

Cluster nodes run on physical or virtual machines. In most cases, the operating system on those machines is a Linux distribution. Evidently, the operating system can expose security vulnerabilities.

Over time, you need to keep the version of the operating system up to date with the latest security fixes. This process could entail upgrading a node's operating system from Ubuntu 18 to 22, for example. Upgrading the operating system is out of scope for this book; for more information, check the relevant Linux documentation.

Many Linux distributions, such as Ubuntu, come with additional tools, applications, and services that are not necessarily required for operating the Kubernetes cluster.

It is your job as an administrator to identify security risks, disable or remove any operating system-specific functionality that may expose vulnerabilities, and keep the operating system patched to incorporate the latest security fixes. The less functionality an operating system has, the smaller the risk.

CIS benchmark for Ubuntu Linux

As a reference guide, you may want to compare your operating system's configuration with the CIS benchmark for Ubuntu Linux (*https://oreil.ly/AeAAE*).

Scenario: An Attacker Exploits a Package Vulnerability

Figure 4-1 illustrates an attacker exploiting a vulnerability of a package installed on the system. For example, the application could be the package manager snapd (*https://oreil.ly/ZOFTj*). Assume that the attacker takes advantage of the known vulnerability USN-5292-1 (*https://oreil.ly/lw_MV*) that has the potential of exposing sensitive information to an attacker.

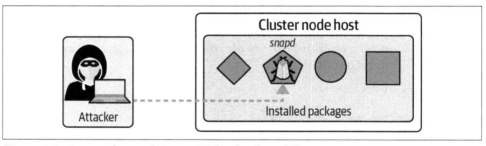

Figure 4-1. An attacker exploits an OS-level vulnerability

The following section will explain how to minimize security risks for services and packages that are not really needed for operating Kubernetes by simply disabling or removing them.

Disabling Services

On Linux, many applications run as services in the background. Services can be managed using the command line tool `systemctl`. The following `systemctl` command lists all running services:

```
$ systemctl | grep running
...
snapd.service    loaded active running   Snap Daemon
```

One of the services we will not need for operating a cluster node is the package manager snapd. For more details on the service, retrieve the status for it with the status subcommand:

```
$ systemctl status snapd
• snapd.service - Snap Daemon
     Loaded: loaded (/lib/systemd/system/snapd.service; enabled; vendor \
     preset: enabled)
     Active: active (running) since Mon 2022-09-19 22:49:56 UTC; 30min ago
TriggeredBy: • snapd.socket
   Main PID: 704 (snapd)
      Tasks: 12 (limit: 2339)
     Memory: 45.9M
     CGroup: /system.slice/snapd.service
             └─704 /usr/lib/snapd/snapd
```

You can stop service using the systemctl subcommand stop:

```
$ sudo systemctl stop snapd
Warning: Stopping snapd.service, but it can still be activated by:
   snapd.socket
```

Execute the disable subcommand to prevent the service from being started again upon a system restart:

```
$ sudo systemctl disable snapd
Removed /etc/systemd/system/multi-user.target.wants/snapd.service.
```

The service has now been stopped and disabled:

```
$ systemctl status snapd
• snapd.service - Snap Daemon
     Loaded: loaded (/lib/systemd/system/snapd.service; disabled; vendor \
     preset: enabled)
     Active: inactive (dead) since Mon 2022-09-19 23:22:22 UTC; 4min 4s ago
TriggeredBy: • snapd.socket
   Main PID: 704 (code=exited, status=0/SUCCESS)
```

Removing Unwanted Packages

Now that the service has been disabled, there's no more point in keeping the package around. You can remove the package to free up additional disk space and memory. You can use the apt purge command to remove a package and its transitive packages, as demonstrated in the following:

```
$ sudo apt purge --auto-remove snapd
Reading package lists... Done
Building dependency tree
Reading state information... Done
The following packages will be REMOVED:
   snapd* squashfs-tools*
0 upgraded, 0 newly installed, 2 to remove and 116 not upgraded.
After this operation, 147 MB disk space will be freed.
```

```
Do you want to continue? [Y/n] y
...
```

You can use the same command even if the package isn't controlled by a service. Identify the packages you don't need and simply remove them. You should end up with a much slimmer footprint of your system.

A potential attacker cannot use the snapd service anymore to exploit the system. You should repeat the process for any unwanted services. As a result, the snapd service ceases to exist on the system:

```
$ systemctl status snapd
Unit snapd.service could not be found.
```

Minimizing IAM Roles

Identity and access management (IAM) on the system level involves management of Linux users, the groups they belong to, and the permissions granted to them. Any directory and file will have file permissions assigned to a user.

Proper user and access management is a classic responsibility of every system administrator. While your role as a Kubernetes administrator may not directly involve system-level IAM, it's important to understand the implications to security. You will likely have to work with a peer to harden the system running the Kubernetes cluster.

This section will provide a short introduction on how to manage users and groups. We will also discuss how to set file permissions and ownership to minimize access as much as possible. We will only scratch the surface of the topic in this book. For more information, refer to the Linux documentation of your choice.

Scenario: An Attacker Uses Credentials to Gain File Access

A security breach can lead to stolen user credentials. Gaining access to valid user credentials opens the door for additional attack vectors. Figure 4-2 shows an attacker who could log into a cluster node with stolen user credentials and can now interact with all files and directories with the permissions granted to the user.

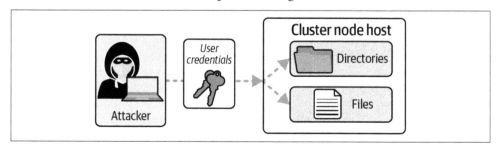

Figure 4-2. An attacker uses stolen credentials to access files

It's recommended to follow the principle of least privilege. Only grant administrative permissions to a limited group of users. All other users should only be allowed to perform operations necessary to perform their jobs.

Understanding User Management

Every user must authenticate to a system to use it. The authenticated user has access to resources based on the assigned permissions. This section will walk you through the primary operations required to manage users.

Listing users

To list all users on the system, render the contents of the file /etc/passwd. Every entry follows the general pattern username:password:UID:GID:comment: home:shell. Some of the fields within the pattern may be empty:

```
$ cat /etc/passwd
root:x:0:0:root:/root:/bin/bash
nobody:x:65534:65534:nobody:/nonexistent:/usr/sbin/nologin
...
```

The command output renders the user root in the first position of the output. The last portion of the string for the root user, /bin/bash, indicates that the user is allowed to log into the system with a bash shell. Other users might not be allowed to log in at all. For those users, you will find the string /usr/sbin/nologin assigned to the shell field.

At any given point of time, you can see which processes have been started by users. The following command shows all bash processes, including the corresponding user that started it:

```
$ ps aux | grep bash
root         956  0.0  0.4  22512 19200 pts/0     Ss   17:57   0:00 -bash
root        7064  0.0  0.0   6608  2296 pts/0     S+   18:08   0:00 grep \
--color=auto bash
```

Adding a user

At some point, you may want to give team members access to the machines running the cluster nodes, with limited permissions. You can add new users to the system with the adduser command. Add the flag --shell /sbin/nologin to disable shell access for the user. The following command creates the user ben:

```
$ sudo adduser ben
Adding user 'ben' ...
Adding new group 'ben' (1001) ...
Adding new user 'ben' (1001) with group 'ben' ...
Creating home directory '/home/ben' ...
Copying files from '/etc/skel' ...
```

```
New password:
Retype new password:
...
```

The user entry has been added to the file /etc/passwd:

```
$ cat /etc/passwd
...
ben:x:1001:1001:,,,:/home/ben:/bin/bash
```

Switching to a user

You can change the user in a shell by using the su command. The following command switches to the user ben we created earlier. You will be asked to enter the user's password:

```
$ su ben
Password:
ben@controlplane:/root$ pwd
/root
```

The shell will indicate the current user by its prompt. You will inherit the environment variables from the account you used when running the su command. To create a new environment, add the hyphen with the su command:

```
$ su - ben
ben@controlplane:~$ pwd
/home/ben
```

Another way to temporarily switch the user is by using the sudo command. You will need to have elevated privileges to execute the command. Therefore, the sudo command is equivalent to "run this command as administrator":

```
$ sudo -u ben pwd
/root
```

Deleting a user

Team members, represented by users in the system, transition to other teams or may simply leave the company. You will want to revoke access to the user to prevent unauthorized use of the credentials. The following command deletes the user, including the user's home directory:

```
$ sudo userdel -r ben
```

Understanding Group Management

It's more convenient for a system administrator to group users with similar access requirements to control permissions on an individual user level. Linux systems offer the concept of a group as a way to organize users based on teams, or specific organizational roles. We'll briefly touch on the most important aspects of group management.

Listing groups

Groups can be listed by inspecting the contents of the file /etc/group. Every entry follows the general pattern groupname:password:GID:group members:

```
$ cat /etc/group
root:x:0:
plugdev:x:46:packer
nogroup:x:65534:
...
```

As you can see in the output, some of the fields may be empty. The only group with an assigned member is plugdev, whose name is packer.

Adding a group

Use the command groupadd to add a new group. The following example adds the group kube-developers:

```
$ sudo groupadd kube-developers
```

The group will now be listed in the file /etc/group. Notice that the group identifier is 1004:

```
$ cat /etc/group
...
kube-developers:x:1004:
```

Assigning a user to a group

To assign a group to a user, use the usermod command. The following command adds the user ben to the group kube-developers:

```
$ sudo usermod -g kube-developers ben
```

The group identifier 1004 acts as a stand-in for the group kube-developers:

```
$ cat /etc/passwd | grep ben
ben:x:1001:1004:,,,:/home/ben:/bin/bash
```

Deleting a group

Sometimes you want to get rid of a group entirely. Maybe the organizational role referring to a Linux group that does not exist anymore. Use the groupdel command to delete a group. You will receive an error message if the members are still part of the group:

```
$ sudo groupdel kube-developers
groupdel: cannot remove the primary group of user ben
```

Before deleting a group, you should reassign group members to a different group using the `usermod` command. The following command changes the group from `kube-developers` to `kube-admins`. Assume that the group `kube-admins` has been created before:

```
$ sudo usermod -g kube-admins ben
$ sudo groupdel kube-developers
```

Understanding File Permissions and Ownership

Assigning the file permissions with as minimal access as possible is crucial to maximizing security. This is where Linux file permissions and ownership come into play. I am only going to discuss the relevant operations on a high level. Refer to the Linux Foundation's blog post about Linux file permissions (*https://oreil.ly/3IpRT*) for more details.

Viewing file permissions and ownership

Every user can create new directories and files. For example, you could use the `touch` command to create an empty file. The following command creates a file with the name `my-file` in the current directory:

```
$ touch my-file
```

To see the contents of a directory in the "long" format, use the `ls` command. The long format of the output requested by the `-l` command line parameter renders the file permissions and the file ownership:

```
$ ls -l
total 0
-rw-r--r-- 1 root root 0 Sep 26 17:53 my-file
```

The important portion of the output is `-rw-r--r--`. The first character is a special permission character that can vary per system, followed by three groupings with the notation `rwx`. The first three characters stand for the owner permissions, the second set of three characters is for the group permissions, and the last three characters represent the permissions for all users. The symbol `r` means read permissions, `w` stands for write permissions, and `x` refers to execution permissions. In the previous example, the user `root` can read and write the file, whereas the group and all other users can only read the file.

Changing file ownership

Use the `chown` command to change the user and group assignment for a file or directory. The syntax of the command follows the pattern `chown owner:group filename`. The following command changes the ownership of the file to the user `ben` but does not reassign a group. The user executing the `chown` command needs to have write permissions:

```
$ chown ben my-file
$ ls -l
total 0
-rw-r--r-- 1 ben  root 0 Sep 26 17:53 my-file
```

Changing file permissions

You can add or remove permissions with the `chmod` command in a variety of notations. For example, use the following command to remove write permissions for the file owner:

```
$ chmod -w file1
$ ls -l
total 0
-r--r--r-- 1 ben  root 0 Sep 26 17:53 my-file
```

Minimizing External Access to the Network

External access to your cluster nodes should only be allowed for the ports necessary to operate Kubernetes. We already discussed the standard Kubernetes ports in "Protecting Node Metadata and Endpoints" on page 28. Access to all other ports should be blocked.

Identifying and Disabling Open Ports

Applications like FTP servers, web servers, and file and print services such as Samba open ports as a means to expose a communication endpoint to clients. Running applications that open network communication can expose a security risk. You can eliminate the risk by simply disabling the service and deinstalling the application.

Let's say we installed the Apache 2 HTTP web server (*https://oreil.ly/t-np3*) on a control plane node with the following commands:

```
$ sudo apt update
$ sudo apt install apache2
```

Update about netstat command

The `netstat` command has been deprecated in favor of the faster, more human-readable `ss` command. For more information, refer to the documentation of the operating system you are using.

We can inspect all open ports using the command line tool `ss`, a utility with similar functionality to `netstat`. The following command renders all of the open ports, including their processes. Among them is port 80, exposed by Apache 2:

```
$ sudo ss -ltpn
State    Recv-Q    Send-Q    Local Address:Port    Peer Address:Port    Process
...
LISTEN   0         511       *:80                  *:*                  users: \
(("apache2",pid=18435,fd=4),("apache2",pid=18434,fd=4),("apache2", ]\
pid=18432,fd=4))
```

You may have only needed the web server temporarily and may have simply forgotten about installing it. The process is currently managed by a server. You can review the status of a service with the `systemctl status` command:

```
$ sudo systemctl status apache2
● apache2.service - The Apache HTTP Server
     Loaded: loaded (/lib/systemd/system/apache2.service; enabled; vendor \
     preset: enabled)
     Active: active (running) since Tue 2022-09-20 22:25:25 UTC; 39s ago
       Docs: https://httpd.apache.org/docs/2.4/
   Main PID: 18432 (apache2)
      Tasks: 55 (limit: 2339)
     Memory: 5.6M
     CGroup: /system.slice/apache2.service
             ├─18432 /usr/sbin/apache2 -k start
             ├─18434 /usr/sbin/apache2 -k start
             └─18435 /usr/sbin/apache2 -k start
```

Apache 2 is not needed by Kubernetes. We decide to shut down the service and deinstall the package:

```
$ sudo systemctl stop apache2
$ sudo systemctl disable apache2
Synchronizing state of apache2.service with SysV service script with \
/lib/systemd/systemd-sysv-install.
Executing: /lib/systemd/systemd-sysv-install disable apache2
Removed /etc/systemd/system/multi-user.target.wants/apache2.service.
$ sudo apt purge --auto-remove apache2
```

Verify that the port isn't used anymore. The `ss` command doesn't find an application exposing port 80 anymore:

```
$ sudo ss -ltpn | grep :80
```

Setting Up Firewall Rules

Another way to control ports is with the help of an operating-system-level firewall. On Linux, you could use the Uncomplicated Firewall (UFW) (*https://oreil.ly/iqiwv*). This section will give you a very brief introduction on how to enable UFW and how to configure firewall rules.

Following the principle of least privilege, it's a good idea to start by enabling the firewall and setting up deny rules for *any* incoming and outgoing network traffic. The following commands demonstrate the steps to achieve that:

```
$ sudo ufw allow ssh
Rules updated
Rules updated (v6)
$ sudo ufw default deny outgoing
Default outgoing policy changed to deny
(be sure to update your rules accordingly)
$ sudo ufw default deny incoming
Default incoming policy changed to deny
(be sure to update your rules accordingly)
$ sudo ufw enable
Command may disrupt existing ssh connections. Proceed with operation (y|n)? y
Firewall is active and enabled on system startup
```

You will want to allow external tools like kubectl to connect to the API server running on port 6443. On the control plane node, execute the following command to allow access to the API server port:

```
$ sudo ufw allow 6443
Rule added
Rule added (v6)
```

You will have to repeat the same process to open up other ports on control plane and worker nodes. Ensure that all other ports not needed to operate Kubernetes are blocked.

Using Kernel Hardening Tools

Applications or processes running inside of a container can make system calls. A typical example could be the curl command performing an HTTP request. A system call is a programmatic abstraction running in the user space for requesting a service from the kernel. We can restrict which system calls are allowed to be made with the help of kernel hardening tools. The CKS exam explicitly mentions two tools in this space, AppArmor and seccomp. We'll discuss both tools and the mechanics to integrate them with Kubernetes.

Using AppArmor

AppArmor (*https://apparmor.net*) provides access control to programs running on a Linux system. The tool implements an additional security layer between the applications invoked in the user space and the underlying system functionality. For example, we can restrict network calls or filesystem interaction. Many Linux distributions (e.g., Debian, Ubuntu, openSUSE) already ship with AppArmor. Therefore, AppArmor doesn't have to be installed manually. Linux distributions that do not support AppArmor use Security-Enhanced Linux (SELinux) (*https://oreil.ly/CKBr7*)

instead, which takes a similar approach to AppArmor. Understanding SELinux is out of scope for the CKS exam.

Understanding profiles

The rules that define what a program can or cannot do are defined in an AppArmor profile. Every profile needs to be loaded into AppArmor before it can take effect. AppArmor provides a command line tool for checking the profiles that have been loaded. Execute the command `aa-status` to see a summary of all loaded profiles. You will see that AppArmor already comes with a set of default application profiles to protect Linux services:

```
$ sudo aa-status
apparmor module is loaded.
31 profiles are loaded.
31 profiles are in enforce mode.
   /snap/snapd/15177/usr/lib/snapd/snap-confine
   ...
0 profiles are in complain mode.
14 processes have profiles defined.
14 processes are in enforce mode.
   /pause (11934) docker-default
   ...
0 processes are in complain mode.
0 processes are unconfined but have a profile defined.
```

The profile mode determines the treatment of rules at runtime should a matching event happen. AppArmor distinguishes two types of profile modes:

Enforce
> The system enforces the rules, reports the violation, and writes it to the syslog. You will want to use this mode to prevent a program from making specific calls.

Complain
> The system does not enforce the rules but will write violations to the log. This mode is helpful if you want to discover the calls a program makes.

Example 4-1 defines a custom profile in the file `k8s-deny-write` for restricting file write access. The file should be placed in the directory `/etc/apparmor.d` of every worker node that executes workload. It is out of scope of this book to explain all the rules in detail. For more information, have a look at the AppArmor wiki (*https://oreil.ly/mNuWB*).

Example 4-1. An AppArmor profile for restricting file write access

```
#include <tunables/global>

profile k8s-deny-write flags=(attach_disconnected) { ❶
```

```
#include <abstractions/base>

file, ❷

deny /** w, ❸
}
```

❶ The identifier after the `profile` keyword is the name of the profile.

❷ Apply to file operations.

❸ Deny all file writes.

Setting a custom profile

To load the profile into AppArmor, run the following command on the worker node:

```
$ sudo apparmor_parser /etc/apparmor.d/k8s-deny-write
```

The command uses the enforce mode by default. To load the profile in complain mode, use the `-C` option. The `aa-status` command will now list the profile in addition to the default profiles. As you can see in the output, the profile is listed in enforce mode:

```
$ sudo aa-status
apparmor module is loaded.
32 profiles are loaded.
32 profiles are in enforce mode.
   k8s-deny-write
   ...
```

AppArmor supports additional convenience commands as part of a utilities package. You can manually install the package using the following commands if you want to use them:

```
$ sudo apt-get update
$ sudo apt-get install apparmor-utils
```

Once installed, you can use the command `aa-enforce` to load a profile in enforce mode, and `aa-complain` to load a profile in complain mode. For the exam, it's likely easier to just go with the standard `apparmor_parser` command.

Applying a profile to a container

You need to ensure a couple of prerequisites before using AppArmor rules in a Pod definition. First, the container runtime needs to support AppArmor to let rules take effect. In addition, AppArmor needs to be installed on the worker node that runs the Pod. Last, make sure you loaded the profile, as described in the previous section.

Example 4-2 shows a YAML manifest for a Pod defined in the file `pod.yaml`. To apply a profile to the container, you will need to set a specific annotation. The annotation key needs to use the key in the format `container.apparmor.security.beta.kubernetes.io/<container-name>`. In our case, the container name is `hello`. The full key is `container.apparmor.security.beta.kubernetes.io/hello`. The value of the annotation follows the pattern `localhost/<profile-name>`. The custom profile we want to use here is `k8s-deny-write`. For more information on the configuration options, see the Kubernetes documentation (*https://oreil.ly/1o3zO*).

Example 4-2. A Pod applying an AppArmor profile to a container

```
apiVersion: v1
kind: Pod
metadata:
  name: hello-apparmor
  annotations:
    container.apparmor.security.beta.kubernetes.io/hello: \ ❶
    localhost/k8s-deny-write ❷
spec:
  containers:
  - name: hello ❸
    image: busybox:1.28
    command: ["sh", "-c", "echo 'Hello AppArmor!' && sleep 1h"]
```

❶ The annotation key that consists of a hard-coded prefix and the container name separated by a slash character.

❷ The profile name available on the current node indicated by `localhost`.

❸ The container name.

We are ready to create the Pod. Run the `apply` command and point it to the YAML manifest. Wait until the Pod transitions into the "Running" status:

```
$ kubectl apply -f pod.yaml
pod/hello-apparmor created
$ kubectl get pod hello-apparmor
NAME             READY   STATUS    RESTARTS   AGE
hello-apparmor   1/1     Running   0          4s
```

You can now shell into the container and perform a file write operation:

```
$ kubectl exec -it hello-apparmor -- /bin/sh
/ # touch test.txt
touch: test.txt: Permission denied
```

AppArmor will prevent writing a file to the container's filesystem. The message "Permission denied" will be rendered if you try to perform the operation.

Using seccomp

Seccomp, short for "Secure Computing Mode," is another Linux kernel feature that can restrict the calls made from the userspace into the kernel. A seccomp profile is the mechanism for defining the rules for restricting syscalls and their arguments. Using seccomp can reduce the risk of exploiting a Linux kernel vulnerability. For more information on seccomp on Kubernetes, see the documentation (*https://oreil.ly/B8I5L*).

Applying the default container runtime profile to a container

Container runtimes, such as Docker Engine or containerd, ship with a default seccomp profile. The default seccomp profile allows the most commonly used syscalls used by applications while at the same time forbidding the use of syscalls considered dangerous.

Kubernetes does not apply the default container runtime profile to containers when creating a Pod, but you can enable it using the `SeccompDefault` feature gate (*https://oreil.ly/m9g0G*). Alternatively, you can opt into the feature on a Pod-by-Pod basis by setting the seccomp profile type to `RuntimeDefault` with the help of the security context attribute `seccompProfile`. Example 4-3 demonstrates its use.

Example 4-3. A Pod applying the default seccomp profile provided by the container runtime profile

```
apiVersion: v1
kind: Pod
metadata:
  name: hello-seccomp
spec:
  securityContext:
    seccompProfile:
      type: RuntimeDefault  ❶
  containers:
  - name: hello
    image: busybox:1.28
    command: ["sh", "-c", "echo 'Hello seccomp!' && sleep 1h"]
```

❶   Applies the default container runtime profile.

You can start the Pod using the `apply` command and point to the YAML manifest. The Pod should transition into the "Running" status:

```
$ kubectl apply -f pod.yaml
pod/hello-seccomp created
$ kubectl get pod hello-seccomp
NAME            READY   STATUS    RESTARTS   AGE
hello-seccomp   1/1     Running   0          4s
```

The echo command executed in the container is considered unproblematic from a security perspective by the default seccomp profile. The following command inspects the logs of the container:

```
$ kubectl logs hello-seccomp
Hello seccomp!
```

The call was permitted and resulted in writing the message "Hello seccomp!" to standard output.

Setting a custom profile

You can create and set your own custom profile in addition to the default container runtime profile. The standard directory for those files is /var/lib/kubelet/seccomp. We'll organize our custom profiles in the subdirectory profiles. Create the directory if it doesn't exist yet:

```
$ sudo mkdir -p /var/lib/kubelet/seccomp/profiles
```

We decide to create our custom profile in the file mkdir-violation.json in the profile directory. Example 4-4 shows the details of the profile definition. In a nutshell, the rule set disallows the use of the mkdir syscall.

Example 4-4. A seccomp profile that prevents executing a mkdir syscall

```
{
    "defaultAction": "SCMP_ACT_ALLOW", ❶
    "architectures": [ ❷
        "SCMP_ARCH_X86_64",
        "SCMP_ARCH_X86",
        "SCMP_ARCH_X32"
    ],
    "syscalls": [
        {
            "names": [
                "mkdir"
            ],
            "action": "SCMP_ACT_ERRNO" ❸
        }
    ]
}
```

❶ The default action applies to all system calls. Here we'll allow all syscalls using SCMP_ACT_ALLOW.

❷ You can filter for specific architectures the default action should apply to. The definition of the field is optional.

❸ The default action can be overwritten by declaring more fine-grained rules. The SCMP_ACT_ERRNO action will prevent the execution of the `mkdir` syscall.

Placing a custom profile into the directory `/var/lib/kubelet/seccomp` doesn't automatically apply the rules to a Pod. You still need to configure a Pod to use it.

Applying the custom profile to a container

Applying a custom profile follows a similar pattern to applying the default container runtime profile, with minor differences. As you can see in Example 4-5, we point the `seccompProfile` attribute of the security profile to the file `mkdir-violation.json` and set the type to `Localhost`.

Example 4-5. A Pod applying a custom seccomp profile prevents a `mkdir` syscall

```
apiVersion: v1
kind: Pod
metadata:
  name: hello-seccomp
spec:
  securityContext:
    seccompProfile:
      type: Localhost ❶
      localhostProfile: profiles/mkdir-violation.json ❷
  containers:
  - name: hello
    image: busybox:1.28
    command: ["sh", "-c", "echo 'Hello seccomp!' && sleep 1h"]
    securityContext:
      allowPrivilegeEscalation: false
```

❶ Refers to a profile on the current node.

❷ Applies the profile with the name `mkdir-violation.json` in the subdirectory `profiles`.

Create the Pod using the declarative `apply` command. Wait until the Pod transitions into the "Running" status:

```
$ kubectl apply -f pod.yaml
pod/hello-seccomp created
$ kubectl get pod hello-seccomp
NAME            READY   STATUS    RESTARTS   AGE
hello-seccomp   1/1     Running   0          4s
```

Shell into the container to verify that seccomp properly enforced the applied rules:

```
$ kubectl exec -it hello-seccomp -- /bin/sh
/ # mkdir test
mkdir: can't create directory test: Operation not permitted
```

As you can see in output, the operation renders an error message when trying to execute the mkdir command. The rule in the custom profile has been violated.

Summary

Addressing security aspects isn't limited to Kubernetes cluster components or workload. There's plenty you can do on the host system level. We discussed different OS capabilities and how to use them to minimize potential security vulnerabilities.

Many operating systems come with a wealth of packages and services to offer a more feature-rich experience to end users. It's important to identify functionality not required to operate a Kubernetes cluster. Purge unnecessary packages and services rigorously and close ports you don't need. You will also want to limited which users are allowed to have access to specific directories, files, and applications. Use Linux's user management to restrict permissions.

It's very common for applications and processes running in containers to make system calls. You can use Linux kernel hardening tools like AppArmor and seccomp to restrict those calls. Only allow system calls crucial to fulfill the needs of your application running the container.

Exam Essentials

Have a basic understanding of Linux OS tooling.
The CKS exam primarily focuses on security functionality in Kubernetes. This domain crosses the boundary to Linux OS security features. It won't hurt to explore Linux-specific tools and security aspects independent from the content covered in this chapter. On a high level, familiarize yourself with service, package, user, and network management on Linux.

Know how to integrate Linux kernel hardening tools with Kubernetes.
AppArmor and seccomp are just some kernel hardening tools that can be integrated with Kubernetes to restrict system calls made from a container. Practice the process of loading a profile and applying it to a container. In order to expand your horizons, you may also want to explore other kernel functionality that works alongside Kubernetes, such as SELinux (*https://oreil.ly/DrGbB*) or sysctl (*https://oreil.ly/GyUoc*).

Sample Exercises

Solutions to these exercises are available in the Appendix.

1. Navigate to the directory *app-a/ch04/close-ports* of the checked-out GitHub repository *bmuschko/cks-study-guide* (*https://oreil.ly/sImXZ*). Start up the VMs running the cluster using the command `vagrant up`. The cluster consists of a single control plane node named `kube-control-plane` and one worker node named `kube-worker-1`. Once done, shut down the cluster using `vagrant destroy -f`.

   Identify the process listening on port 21 in the VM `kube-worker-1`. You decided not to expose this port to reduce the risk of attackers exploiting the port. Close the port by shutting down the corresponding process.

   Prerequisite: This exercise requires the installation of the tools Vagrant (*https:// oreil.ly/FiyeH*) and VirtualBox (*https://oreil.ly/WW8IK*).

2. Navigate to the directory *app-a/ch04/apparmor* of the checked-out GitHub repository *bmuschko/cks-study-guide* (*https://oreil.ly/sImXZ*). Start up the VMs running the cluster using the command `vagrant up`. The cluster consists of a single control plane node named `kube-control-plane`, and one worker node named `kube-worker-1`. Once done, shut down the cluster using `vagrant destroy -f`.

   Create an AppArmor profile named `network-deny`. The profile should prevent any incoming and outgoing network traffic. Add the profile to the set of AppArmor rules in enforce mode. Apply the profile to the Pod named `network-call` running in the `default` namespace. Check the logs of the Pod to ensure that network calls cannot be made anymore.

   Prerequisite: This exercise requires the installation of the tools Vagrant (*https:// oreil.ly/FiyeH*) and VirtualBox (*https://oreil.ly/WW8IK*).

3. Navigate to the directory *app-a/ch04/seccomp* of the checked-out GitHub repository *bmuschko/cks-study-guide* (*https://oreil.ly/sImXZ*). Start up the VMs running the cluster using the command `vagrant up`. The cluster consists of a single control plane node named `kube-control-plane`, and one worker node named `kube-worker-1`. Once done, shut down the cluster using `vagrant destroy -f`.

   Create a seccomp profile file named `audit.json` that logs all syscalls in the standard seccomp directory. Apply the profile to the Pod named `network-call` running in the `default` namespace. Check the log file `/var/log/syslog` for log entries.

   Prerequisite: This exercise requires the installation of the tools Vagrant (*https:// oreil.ly/FiyeH*) and VirtualBox (*https://oreil.ly/WW8IK*).

4. Create a new Pod named `sysctl-pod` with the image `nginx:1.23.1`. Set the sysctl parameters `net.core.somaxconn` to 1024 and `debug.iotrace` to 1. Check on the status of the Pod.

Minimizing Microservice Vulnerabilities

Application stacks operated in a Kubernetes cluster often follow a microservices architecture. The domain "minimize microservice vulnerabilities" covers governance and enforcement of security settings on the Pod level. We'll touch on Kubernetes core features, as well as external tooling, that help with minimizing security vulnerabilities. Additionally, we'll also talk about encrypted network communication between Pods running microservices.

At a high level, this chapter covers the following concepts:

- Setting up appropriate OS-level security domains with security contexts, Pod Security Admission (PSA), and Open Policy Agent Gatekeeper

- Managing Secrets

- Using container runtime sandboxes, such as gVisor and Kata Containers

- Implementing Pod-to-Pod communication encryption via mutual Transport Layer Security (TLS)

Setting Appropriate OS-Level Security Domains

Both core Kubernetes and the Kubernetes ecosystem offer solutions for defining, enforcing, and governing security settings on the Pod and container level. This section will discuss security contexts, Pod Security Admission, and Open Policy Agent Gatekeeper. You will learn how to apply each of the features and tools using examples that demonstrate their importance to security. Let's begin by setting up a scenario.

Scenario: An Attacker Misuses root User Container Access

By default, containers run with root privileges. A vulnerability in the application could grant an attacker root access to the container. The container's root user is the same as the root user on the host machine. Not only can the attacker then inspect or modify the application, but they can also potentially install additional tooling that allows the attacker to break out of the container and step into host namespace with root permissions. The attacker could also copy sensitive data from the host's filesystem to the container. Figure 5-1 illustrates the scenario.

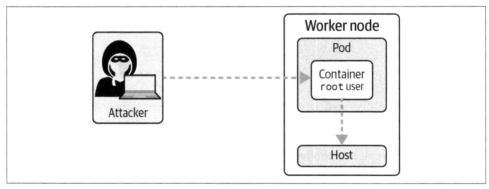

Figure 5-1. An attacker misuses root user container access

For that reason, running a container with the default root user is a bad idea. The next sections will explain how to declare a security context for the container that enforces the use of a non-root user or a specific user and/or group identifier. We'll also discuss other security context settings relevant to shielding host access from the container.

Understanding Security Contexts

Kubernetes, as the container orchestration engine, can apply additional configuration to increase container security. You do so by defining a security context. A security context defines privilege and access control settings for a Pod or a container. The following list provides some examples:

- The user ID that should be used to run the Pod and/or container
- The group ID that should be used for filesystem access
- Granting a running process inside the container some privileges of the root user but not all of them

The security context is not a Kubernetes primitive. It is modeled as a set of attributes under the directive `securityContext` within the Pod specification. Security settings defined on the Pod level apply to all containers running in the Pod; however, container-level settings take precedence. For more information on Pod-level security attributes, see the PodSecurityContext API (*https://oreil.ly/cJWXA*). Container-level security attributes can be found in the SecurityContext API (*https://oreil.ly/XOy2a*).

Enforcing the Usage of a Non-Root User

We'll have a look at a use case to make the functionality more transparent. Some images, like the one for the open source reverse-proxy server nginx, must be run with the `root` user. Say you wanted to enforce that containers cannot be run as the `root` user as a means to support a more sensible security strategy. The YAML manifest file `container-non-root-user-error.yaml` shown in Example 5-1 defines the security configuration specifically for a container. This security context only applies to this very container, but not others if you were to define more.

Example 5-1. Enforcing a non-root user on an image that needs to run with the root user

```
apiVersion: v1
kind: Pod
metadata:
  name: non-root-error
spec:
  containers:
  - image: nginx:1.23.1
    name: nginx
    securityContext:
      runAsNonRoot: true
```

The container fails during the startup process with the status `CreateContainer ConfigError`. A look at the Pod's event log reveals that the image tries to run with the `root` user. The configured security context does not allow it:

```
$ kubectl apply -f container-non-root-user-error.yaml
pod/non-root-error created
$ kubectl get pod non-root-error
NAME             READY   STATUS                     RESTARTS   AGE
non-root-error   0/1     CreateContainerConfigError   0          9s
$ kubectl describe pod non-root-error
...
Events:
  Type     Reason      Age                     From               Message
  ----     ------      ----                    ----               -------
  Normal   Scheduled   24s                     default-scheduler  Successfully \
  assigned default/non-root to minikube
  Normal   Pulling     24s                     kubelet            Pulling image \
  "nginx:1.23.1"
  Normal   Pulled      16s                     kubelet            Successfully \
  pulled image "nginx:1.23.1" in 7.775950615s
```

```
Warning   Failed     4s (x3 over 16s)  kubelet              Error: container \
has runAsNonRoot and image will run as root (pod: "non-root-error_default \
(6ed9ed71-1002-4dc2-8cb1-3423f86bd144)", container: secured-container)
Normal    Pulled     4s (x2 over 16s)  kubelet              Container image \
"nginx:1.23.1" already present on machine
```

There are alternative nginx container images available that are not required to run
with the root user. An example is bitnami/nginx (*https://oreil.ly/EnvzT*). Example 5-2
shows the contents of the file container-non-root-user-success.yaml. The major
change in this file is the value assigned to the spec.containers[].image attribute.

*Example 5-2. Enforcing a non-root user on an image that supports running with a user
ID*

```
apiVersion: v1
kind: Pod
metadata:
  name: non-root-success
spec:
  containers:
  - image: bitnami/nginx:1.23.1
    name: nginx
    securityContext:
      runAsNonRoot: true
```

Starting the container with the runAsNonRoot directive will work just fine. The
container transitions into the "Running" status:

```
$ kubectl apply -f container-non-root-user-success.yaml
pod/non-root-success created
$ kubectl get pod non-root-success
NAME                READY   STATUS    RESTARTS   AGE
non-root-success    1/1     Running   0          7s
```

Let's quickly check which user ID the container runs with. Shell into the container
and run the id command. The output renders the user ID, the group ID, and the IDs
of supplemental groups. The image bitnami/nginx sets the user ID to 1001 with the
help of an instruction when the container image is built:

```
$ kubectl exec non-root-success -it -- /bin/sh
$ id
uid=1001 gid=0(root) groups=0(root)
$ exit
```

Setting a Specific User and Group ID

Many container images do not set an explicit user ID or group ID. Instead of
running with the root default user, you can set the desired user ID and group
ID to minimize potential security risks. The YAML manifest stored in the file

`container-user-id.yaml` shown in Example 5-3 sets the user ID to 1000 and the group ID to 3000.

Example 5-3. Running the container with a specific user and group ID

```
apiVersion: v1
kind: Pod
metadata:
  name: user-id
spec:
  containers:
  - image: busybox:1.35.0
    name: busybox
    command: ["sh", "-c", "sleep 1h"]
    securityContext:
      runAsUser: 1000
      runAsGroup: 3000
```

Creating the Pod will work without issues. The container transitions into the "Running" status:

```
$ kubectl apply -f container-user-id.yaml
pod/user-id created
$ kubectl get pods user-id
NAME       READY   STATUS    RESTARTS   AGE
user-id    1/1     Running   0          6s
```

You can inspect the user ID and group ID after shelling into the container. The current user is not allowed to create files in the / directory. Creating a file in the /tmp directory will work, as most users have the permissions to write to it:

```
$ kubectl exec user-id -it -- /bin/sh
/ $ id
uid=1000 gid=3000 groups=3000
/ $ touch test.txt
touch: test.txt: Permission denied
/ $ touch /tmp/test.txt
/ $ exit
```

Avoiding Privileged Containers

Kubernetes establishes a clear separation between the container namespace and the host namespace for processes, network, mounts, user ID, and more. You can configure the container's security context to gain privileges to certain aspects of the host namespace. Assume the following implications when using a privileged container:

- Processes within a container almost have the same privileges as processes on the host.

- The container has access to all devices on the host.

- The root user in the container has similar privileges to the root user on the host.

- All directories on the host's filesystem can be mounted in the container.

- Kernel settings can be changed, e.g., by using the sysctl command (*https://oreil.ly/YEcOs*).

Using containers in privileged mode

Configuring a container to use privileged mode should be a rare occasion. Most applications and processes running in a container do not need elevated privileges beyond the container namespace. Should you encounter a Pod that has been configured to use privileged mode, contact the team or developer in charge to clarify, as it will open a loophole for attackers to gain access to the host system.

Let's compare the behavior of a non-privileged container with one configured to run in privileged mode. First, we are going to set up a regular Pod, as shown in Example 5-4. No security context has been set on the Pod or container level.

Example 5-4. A Pod with a container in non-privileged mode

```
apiVersion: v1
kind: Pod
metadata:
  name: non-privileged
spec:
  containers:
  - image: busybox:1.35.0
    name: busybox
    command: ["sh", "-c", "sleep 1h"]
```

Create the Pod and ensure that it comes up properly:

```
$ kubectl apply -f non-privileged.yaml
pod/non-privileged created
$ kubectl get pods
NAME             READY   STATUS    RESTARTS   AGE
non-privileged   1/1     Running   0          6s
```

To demonstrate the isolation between the container namespace and host's namespace, we'll try to use the sysctl to change the hostname. As you can see in the output of the command, the container will clearly enforce the restricted privileges:

```
$ kubectl exec non-privileged -it -- /bin/sh
/ # sysctl kernel.hostname=test
sysctl: error setting key 'kernel.hostname': Read-only file system
/ # exit
```

To make a container privileged, simply assign the value `true` to the security context attribute `privileged`. The YAML manifest in Example 5-5 shows an example.

Example 5-5. A Pod with a container configured to run in privileged mode

```
apiVersion: v1
kind: Pod
metadata:
  name: privileged
spec:
  containers:
  - image: busybox:1.35.0
    name: busybox
    command: ["sh", "-c", "sleep 1h"]
    securityContext:
      privileged: true
```

Create the Pod as usual. The Pod should transition into the "Running" status:

```
$ kubectl apply -f privileged.yaml
pod/privileged created
$ kubectl get pod privileged
NAME         READY   STATUS     RESTARTS   AGE
privileged   1/1     Running    0          6s
```

You can now see that the same `sysctl` will allow you to change the hostname:

```
$ kubectl exec privileged -it -- /bin/sh
/ # sysctl kernel.hostname=test
kernel.hostname = test
/ # exit
```

A container security context configuration related to privileged mode is the attribute `allowPrivilegeEscalation`. This attribute will allow a process running the container to gain more privileges than the parent process. The default value for the attribute is `false`, but if you see the attribute set to `true`, critically question its use. In most cases, you do not need the functionality.

Scenario: A Developer Doesn't Follow Pod Security Best Practices

It is unfair to assume that developers of all trades and levels of seniority have extensive knowledge of Kubernetes features, especially the ones that apply to security best practices. In the previous section, we learned about the security context and which settings to avoid. Developers are probably unaware of those best practices without continued education and therefore may create Pods that use problematic security settings or none at all. Figure 5-2 shows a developer creating a Pod in privileged mode enabled by a copied manifest found on the internet. An attacker will gladly use this setup to their advantage.

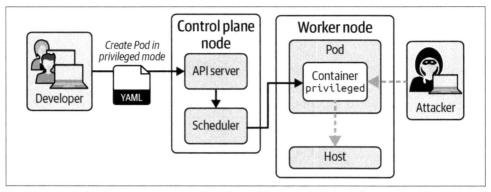

Figure 5-2. A developer creates a Pod with enabled privileged mode

This is where you, as the Kubernetes security specialist, come in. The Kubernetes eco-system provides core features and external tooling for enforcing security standards for Pods so that objects without the right configuration will be rejected, or at least audited. The next section explores the Kubernetes core feature named Pod Security Admission.

Understanding Pod Security Admission (PSA)

Older versions of Kubernetes shipped with a feature called Pod Security Policies (PSP). Pod Security Policies are a concept that help with enforcing security standards for Pod objects. Kubernetes 1.21 deprecated Pod Security Policies and introduced the replacement functionality Pod Security Admission. PSA determines which Pod Security Standard (PSS) to follow. A PSS defines a range of security policies from highly restrictive to highly permissive.

However, the Kubernetes release 1.25 completely removed Pod Security Policies. You may still see the feature listed in older versions of the CKS curriculum. We will only focus on Pod Security Admission in this book. PSA is enabled by default with Kubernetes 1.23; however, you will need to declare which Pods should adhere to the security standards. All you need to do to opt into the PSA feature is to add a label with a specific format to a namespace. All Pods in that namespace will have to follow the standards declared.

The label consists of three parts: a prefix, a mode, and a level. The *prefix* always uses the hard-coded value `pod-security.kubernetes.io` followed by a slash. The *mode* determines the handling of a violation. Finally, the *level* dictates the degree of security standards to adhere to. An example of such a label could look as follows:

```
metadata:
  labels:
    pod-security.kubernetes.io/enforce: restricted
```

The mode allows for setting three different options, shown in Table 5-1.

Table 5-1. Pod Security Admission modes

Mode	Behavior
enforce	Violations will cause the Pod to be rejected.
audit	Pod creation will be allowed. Violations will be appended to the audit log.
warn	Pod creation will be allowed. Violations will be rendered on the console.

Table 5-2 illustrates the security policies determined by the level set for the PSA.

Table 5-2. Pod Security Admission levels

Level	Behavior
privileged	Fully unrestricted policy.
baseline	Minimally restrictive policy that covers crucial standards.
restricted	Heavily restricted policy following best practices for hardening Pods from a security perspective.

See the Kubernetes documentation (*https://oreil.ly/DYziy*) for details on the PSA, including usage examples.

Enforcing Pod Security Standards for a Namespace

Let's apply a PSA to a Pod in the namespace psa. Example 5-6 shows the definition of the namespace and the declaration of the relevant label. The label will enforce a PSS on the highest level of security standards.

Example 5-6. A namespace enforcing the highest level of security standards

```
apiVersion: v1
kind: Namespace
metadata:
  name: psa
  labels:
    pod-security.kubernetes.io/enforce: restricted
```

Make sure that the Pod is created in the namespace psa. Example 5-7 shows the YAML manifest for a simple Pod running the busybox image.

Example 5-7. A Pod violating the PSA restrictions

```
apiVersion: v1
kind: Pod
metadata:
  name: busybox
```

```
    namespace: psa
spec:
  containers:
  - image: busybox:1.35.0
    name: busybox
    command: ["sh", "-c", "sleep 1h"]
```

Violations will be rendered in the console upon running a command to create a Pod in the namespace. As you can see in the following, the Pod wasn't allowed to be created:

```
$ kubectl create -f psa-namespace.yaml
namespace/psa created
$ kubectl apply -f psa-violating-pod.yaml
Error from server (Forbidden): error when creating "psa-pod.yaml": pods \
"busybox" is forbidden: violates PodSecurity "restricted:latest": \
allowPrivilegeEscalation != false (container "busybox" must set \
securityContext.allowPrivilegeEscalation=false), unrestricted \
capabilities (container "busybox" must set securityContext. \
capabilities.drop=["ALL"]), runAsNonRoot != true (pod or container \
"busybox" must set securityContext.runAsNonRoot=true), seccompProfile \
(pod or container "busybox" must set securityContext.seccompProfile. \
type to "RuntimeDefault" or "Localhost")
$ kubectl get pod -n psa
No resources found in psa namespace.
```

You need to configure the Pod's security context settings to follow the very restrictive standards. Example 5-8 shows an exemplary Pod definition that does not violate the Pod Security Standard.

Example 5-8. A Pod following the PSS

```
apiVersion: v1
kind: Pod
metadata:
  name: busybox
  namespace: psa
spec:
  containers:
  - image: busybox:1.35.0
    name: busybox
    command: ["sh", "-c", "sleep 1h"]
    securityContext:
      allowPrivilegeEscalation: false
      capabilities:
        drop: ["ALL"]
      runAsNonRoot: true
      runAsUser: 2000
      runAsGroup: 3000
      seccompProfile:
        type: RuntimeDefault
```

Creating the Pod object now works as expected:

```
$ kubectl apply -f psa-non-violating-pod.yaml
pod/busybox created
$ kubectl get pod busybox -n psa
NAME        READY    STATUS     RESTARTS    AGE
busybox     1/1      Running    0           10s
```

PSA is a built-in, enabled-by-default feature in Kubernetes version 1.23 or higher. It's easy to adopt, allows for picking and choosing a suitable policy standard, and can be configured to enforce or just log violations.

Unfortunately, PSA only applies to Pods with a predescribed set of policies. You cannot write your own custom rules, change the messaging, or mutate the Pod object should it not adhere to a PSS. In the next section, we are going to have a look at tooling that goes beyond the functionality of PSA.

Understanding Open Policy Agent (OPA) and Gatekeeper

Open Policy Agent (OPA) (*https://oreil.ly/oK9pI*) is an open source, general-purpose policy engine for enforcing rules. OPA is not specific to Kubernetes and can be used across other technology stacks. One of its benefits is the ability to define a policy in a very flexible fashion. You can write your own rules with the help of the query language named Rego (*https://oreil.ly/0_mA8*). The validation logic written in Rego determines if the object is accepted or denied.

Gatekeeper (*https://oreil.ly/AyVjP*) is an extension to Kubernetes that uses OPA. Gatekeeper allows for defining and enforcing custom policies for any kind of Kubernetes API primitive. Therefore, it is far more versatile than PSA but requires more intricate knowledge on how to craft those rules. Gatekeeper gets involved in the *admission control* stage discussed in "Processing a Request" on page 44. The following list of policies tries to give you an impression on what's possible with Gatekeeper:

- Ensuring that all Service objects need to define a label with the key `team`
- Ensuring that all container images defined by Pods need to be pulled from a company-internal registry
- Ensuring that Deployments need to control at least three replicas

At the time of writing, Gatekeeper allows for enforcing policies by rejecting object creation if requirements haven't been met. Future versions of Gatekeeper might also provide a mechanism for mutating an object upon creation. For example, you may want to add specific label key-value pairs for any object created. The mutation would take care of adding those labels automatically.

Installing Gatekeeper

Installing Gatekeeper is relatively easy. All you need to do is to create a bunch of Kubernetes objects from a YAML manifest provided by the Gatekeeper project. You need to have cluster admin permissions to properly install Gatekeeper. The following command shows the kubectl command used to apply the latest release. For more information, see the installation manual (*https://oreil.ly/CyZ1c*):

```
$ kubectl apply -f https://raw.githubusercontent.com/open-policy-agent/\
gatekeeper/master/deploy/gatekeeper.yaml
```

Gatekeeper objects have been installed in the namespace gatekeeper-system. Make sure that all Pods in the namespace transition into the "Running" status before trying to use Gatekeeper:

```
$ kubectl get namespaces
NAME                 STATUS    AGE
default              Active    29h
gatekeeper-system    Active    4s
...
```

Implementing an OPA Policy

We'll use a specific use case as an example to demonstrate the moving parts required to define a custom OPA policy. "Using Network Policies to Restrict Pod-to-Pod Communication" on page 11 explained how to assign a label to a namespace so that it can be selected from a network policy. At its core, our custom OPA policy will determine that namespaces need to define at least one label with the key app to signify the application hosted by the namespace.

Gatekeeper requires us to implement two components for custom policy, the *constraint template* and the *constraint*. In a nutshell, the constraint template defines the rules with Rego and describes the schema for the constraint. Example 5-9 shows a constraint template definition for enforcing a label assignment.

Example 5-9. An OPA constraint template requiring the definition of at least a single label

```
apiVersion: templates.gatekeeper.sh/v1
kind: ConstraintTemplate
metadata:
  name: k8srequiredlabels
spec:
  crd:
    spec:
      names:
        kind: K8sRequiredLabels  ❶
      validation:
```

```
          openAPIV3Schema: ❷
            type: object
            properties:
              labels:
                type: array
                items:
                  type: string
  targets:
    - target: admission.k8s.gatekeeper.sh
      rego: | ❸
        package k8srequiredlabels

        violation[{"msg": msg, "details": {"missing_labels": missing}}] {
          provided := {label | input.review.object.metadata.labels[label]}
          required := {label | label := input.parameters.labels[_]}
          missing := required - provided
          count(missing) > 0
          msg := sprintf("you must provide labels: %v", [missing])
        }
```

❶ Declares the kind to be used by the constraint.

❷ Specifies the validation schema of the constraint. In this case, we allow to pass in a property named labels that captures the required label keys.

❸ Uses Rego to check for the existence of labels and compares them to the list of required keys.

The constraint is essentially an implementation of the constraint template. It uses the kind defined by the constraint template and populates the data provided by the end user. In Example 5-10, the kind is K8sRequiredLabels, which we defined in the constraint template. We are matching on namespaces and expect them to define the label with the key app.

Example 5-10. An OPA constraint that defines the "data" for the policy

```
apiVersion: constraints.gatekeeper.sh/v1beta1
kind: K8sRequiredLabels ❶
metadata:
  name: ns-must-have-app-label-key
spec:
  match: ❷
    kinds:
      - apiGroups: [""]
        kinds: ["Namespace"]
  parameters: ❸
    labels: ["app"]
```

❶ Uses the kind defined by the constraint template.

❷ Defines the API resources the constraint template should apply to.

❸ Declares that the labels property expects the key app to exist.

With the relevant YAML manifests in place, let's create the objects for the constraint template and the constraint. Assume that the constraint template was written to the file constraint-template-labels.yaml and the constraint to the file constraint-ns-labels.yaml:

```
$ kubectl apply -f constraint-template-labels.yaml
constrainttemplate.templates.gatekeeper.sh/k8srequiredlabels created
$ kubectl apply -f constraint-ns-labels.yaml
k8srequiredlabels.constraints.gatekeeper.sh/ns-must-have-app-label-key created
```

You can verify the validation behavior with a quick-to-run imperative command. The following command tries to create a new namespace without a label assignment. Gatekeeper will render an error message and prevent the creation of the object:

```
$ kubectl create ns governed-ns
Error from server (Forbidden): admission webhook "validation.gatekeeper.sh" \
denied the request: [ns-must-have-app-label-key] you must provide labels: {"app"}
```

Let's make sure that we can actually create a namespace with the expected label assignment. Example 5-11 shows the YAML manifest of such a namespace.

Example 5-11. YAML manifest for namespace with a label assignment

```
apiVersion: v1
kind: Namespace
metadata:
  labels:
    app: orion
  name: governed-ns
```

The following command creates the object from the YAML manifest file named namespace-app-label.yaml:

```
$ kubectl apply -f namespace-app-label.yaml
namespace/governed-ns created
```

This simple example demonstrated the usage of OPA Gatekeeper. You can find a lot of other examples in the OPA Gatekeeper Library (*https://oreil.ly/1VV5e*). Despite it not being spelled out explicitly in the CKS curriculum, you may also want to check out the project Kyverno (*https://kyverno.io*), which recently gained a lot of traction with the Kubernetes community.

Managing Secrets

No discussion on security features in Kubernetes would be complete without bringing up the topic of Secrets. I would assume that you are already well familiar with the API primitive Secret to define sensitive data and the different options for consuming it in a Pod. Given that this topic is already part of the CKA exam, I will not reiterate it here. For more information, see the relevant section in the *Certified Kubernetes Administrator (CKA) Study Guide* or the Kubernetes documentation (*https://oreil.ly/ 1afoc*). I talk about security aspects when consuming ConfigMaps and Secrets in a container in "Configuring a Container with a ConfigMap or Secret" on page 152.

The CKS exam puts a stronger emphasis on more specialized aspects of Secret management. One of those scenarios, which we already touched on, was the handling of a Secret you can assign to a service account. Revisit "Creating a Secret for a service account" on page 58 to refresh your memory on the topic. As we are not going to discuss all built-in Secret types here, you may want to read up on their purpose and creation in the relevant section of the Kubernetes documentation (*https://oreil.ly/ YU7Yy*).

The central location for storing Secrets key-value pairs is etcd. Let's have a look at potential issues that may arise if an attacker gains access to Kubernetes backing store for cluster data.

Scenario: An Attacker Gains Access to the Node Running etcd

Where etcd runs is dependent on the topology of your Kubernetes cluster (*https:// oreil.ly/bf5Gt*). For the purpose of this scenario, we'll assume that etcd runs on the control plane node. Any data stored in etcd exists in unencrypted form, so access to the control plane node allows for reading Secrets in plain text. Figure 5-3 shows an attacker gaining access to the control plane node and therefore the unencrypted Secrets in etcd.

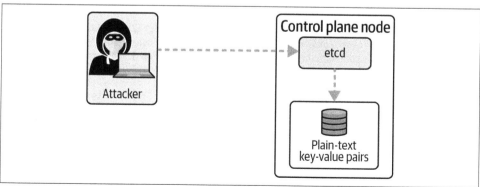

Figure 5-3. An attacker gains access to etcd to read Secrets

One way to mitigate the situation is by encrypting the data stored in etcd. Access to etcd, either using `etcdctl` or by reading the etcd data from the filesystem, would not expose human-readable, sensitive information anymore.

Accessing etcd Data

We'll start by showing how an attacker could read etcd data after being able to log into the control plane node. First, we need to create a Secret object to store in etcd. Use the following imperative command to create an entry:

```
$ kubectl create secret generic app-config --from-literal=password=passwd123
secret/app-config created
```

We created a Secret with the key-value pair `password=passwd123`. Shell into the control plane node using SSH. You can easily use the etcd client tool `etcdctl` to read an entry from etcd.

Using the etcd client tool etcdctl

It's very likely that you do not have `etcdctl` installed on the control plane node yet. Follow the installation manual (*https://oreil.ly/wpCkO*) to make the tool available. On Debian Linux, it can be installed with `sudo apt install etcd-client`. To authenticate against etcd, you will need to provide the mandatory command line options `--cacert`, `--cert`, and `--key`. You can find the corresponding values in the configuration file for the API server usually available at `/etc/kubernetes/manifests/kube-apiserver.yaml`. The parameters need to start with the prefix `--etcd`.

The following command uses the mandatory CLI options to read the contents from the Secret object named `app-config`. The following output displays the file contents in hexadecimal format. While not 100% obvious, you can still identify the key-value pair in plain text from the output:

```
$ sudo ETCDCTL_API=3 etcdctl --cacert=/etc/kubernetes/pki/etcd/ca.crt \
--cert=/etc/kubernetes/pki/etcd/server.crt --key=/etc/kubernetes/pki/\
etcd/server.key get /registry/secrets/default/app-config | hexdump -C
00000000  2f 72 65 67 69 73 74 72  79 2f 73 65 63 72 65 74  |/registry/secret|
00000010  73 2f 64 65 66 61 75 6c  74 2f 61 70 70 2d 63 6f  |s/default/app-co|
00000020  6e 66 69 67 0a 6b 38 73  00 0a 0c 0a 02 76 31 12  |nfig.k8s.....v1.|
00000030  06 53 65 63 72 65 74 12  d9 01 0a b7 01 0a 0a 61  |.Secret........a|
00000040  70 70 2d 63 6f 6e 66 69  67 12 00 1a 07 64 65 66  |pp-config....def|
00000050  61 75 6c 74 22 00 2a 24  36 38 64 65 65 34 34 38  |ault".*$68dee448|
00000060  2d 34 39 62 37 2d 34 34  32 66 2d 39 62 32 66 2d  |-49b7-442f-9b2f-|
00000070  33 66 39 62 39 62 32 61  66 66 36 64 32 00 38 00  |3f9b9b2aff6d2.8.|
00000080  42 08 08 97 f8 a4 9b 06  10 00 7a 00 8a 01 65 0a  |B.........z...e.|
00000090  0e 6b 75 62 65 63 74 6c  2d 63 72 65 61 74 65 12  |.kubectl-create.|
000000a0  06 55 70 64 61 74 65 1a  02 76 31 22 08 08 97 f8  |.Update..v1"....|
```

```
000000b0  a4 9b 06 10 00 32 08 46  69 65 6c 64 73 56 31 3a  |.....2.FieldsV1:|
000000c0  31 0a 2f 7b 22 66 3a 64  61 74 61 22 3a 7b 22 2e  |1./{"f:data":{".|
000000d0  22 3a 7b 7d 2c 22 66 3a  70 61 73 73 77 6f 72 64  |":{},"f:password|
000000e0  22 3a 7b 7d 7d 2c 22 66  3a 74 79 70 65 22 3a 7b  |":{}},"f:type":{|
000000f0  7d 7d 42 00 12 15 0a 08  70 61 73 73 77 6f 72 64  |}}B.....password|
00000100  12 09 70 61 73 73 77 64  31 32 33 1a 06 4f 70 61  |..passwd123..Opa|
00000110  71 75 65 1a 00 22 00 0a                           |que..".. |
```

In the next step, we'll encrypt the Secret stored in etcd and then verify the existing entries with the same command.

Encrypting etcd Data

You can control how API data is encrypted in etcd with the help of the command line option --encryption-provider-config provided to the API server process. The value assigned to the parameter needs to point to a configuration file that defines an EncryptionConfiguration object. We'll first create the configuration file and then configure the API server process to consume it.

Generate a 32-byte random key and base64-encode it. The value is needed to configure a so-called provider in the encryption configuration:

```
$ head -c 32 /dev/urandom | base64
W68xlPT/VXcOSEZJvWeIvkGJnGfQNFpvZYfT9e+ZYuY=
```

Next up, we'll use the base64-encoded key and assign it to a provider in the encryption configuration, as shown in Example 5-12. Save the contents in the file /etc/kubernetes/enc/enc.yaml.

Example 5-12. YAML manifest for encryption configuration

```
apiVersion: apiserver.config.k8s.io/v1
kind: EncryptionConfiguration
resources:
  - resources:
      - secrets ❶
    providers:
      - aescbc:
          keys:
            - name: key1
              secret: W68xlPT/VXcOSEZJvWeIvkGJnGfQNFpvZYfT9e+ZYuY= ❷
      - identity: {}
```

❶ Defines the API resource to be encrypted in etcd. We are only encrypting Secrets data here.

❷ The base64-encoded key assigned to an AES-CBC encryption provider.

Edit the manifest at /etc/kubernetes/manifests/kube-apiserver.yaml, the YAML manifest that defines how to run an API server in a Pod. Add the parameter --encryption-provider-config, and define the Volume and its mountpath for the configuration file as the following shows:

```
$ sudo vim /etc/kubernetes/manifests/kube-apiserver.yaml
apiVersion: v1
kind: Pod
metadata:
  annotations:
    kubeadm.kubernetes.io/kube-apiserver.advertise-address.endpoint: \
    192.168.56.10:6443
  creationTimestamp: null
  labels:
    component: kube-apiserver
    tier: control-plane
  name: kube-apiserver
  namespace: kube-system
spec:
  containers:
  - command:
    - kube-apiserver
    - --encryption-provider-config=/etc/kubernetes/enc/enc.yaml
    volumeMounts:
    ...
    - name: enc
      mountPath: /etc/kubernetes/enc
      readonly: true
    volumes:
    ...
    - name: enc
      hostPath:
        path: /etc/kubernetes/enc
        type: DirectoryOrCreate
  ...
```

The Pod running the API server should automatically restart. This process may take a couple of minutes. Once fully restarted, you should be able to query for it:

```
$ kubectl get pods -n kube-system
NAME                          READY   STATUS    RESTARTS   AGE
...
kube-apiserver-control-plane  1/1     Running   0          69s
```

New Secrets will be encrypted automatically. Existing Secrets need to be updated. You can run the following command to perform an update on Secrets across all namespaces. This includes the Secret named app-config in the default namespace:

```
$ kubectl get secrets --all-namespaces -o json | kubectl replace -f -
...
secret/app-config replaced
```

Running the `etcdctl` command we used before will reveal that the `aescbc` provider has been used to encrypt the data. The password value cannot be read in plain text anymore:

```
$ sudo ETCDCTL_API=3 etcdctl --cacert=/etc/kubernetes/pki/etcd/ca.crt \
--cert=/etc/kubernetes/pki/etcd/server.crt --key=/etc/kubernetes/pki/\
etcd/server.key get /registry/secrets/default/app-config | hexdump -C
00000000  2f 72 65 67 69 73 74 72  79 2f 73 65 63 72 65 74  |/registry/secret|
00000010  73 2f 64 65 66 61 75 6c  74 2f 61 70 70 2d 63 6f  |s/default/app-co|
00000020  6e 66 69 67 0a 6b 38 73  3a 65 6e 63 3a 61 65 73  |nfig.k8s:enc:aes|
00000030  63 62 63 3a 76 31 3a 6b  65 79 31 3a ae 26 e9 c2  |cbc:v1:key1:.&..|
00000040  7b fd a2 74 30 24 85 61  3c 18 1e 56 00 a1 24 65  |{..t0$.a<..V..$e|
00000050  52 3c 3f f1 24 43 9f 6d  de 5f b0 84 32 18 84 47  |R<?.$C.m._..2..G|
00000060  d5 30 e9 64 84 22 f5 d0  0b 6f 02 af db 1d 51 34  |.0.d."...o....Q4|
00000070  db 57 c8 17 93 ed 9e 00  ea 9a 7b ec 0e 75 0c 49  |.W........{..u.I|
00000080  6a e9 97 cd 54 d4 ae 6b  b6 cb 65 8a 5d 4c 3c 9c  |j...T..k..e.]L<.|
00000090  db 9b ed bc ce bf 3c ef  f6 2e cb 6d a2 53 25 49  |......<....m.S%I|
000000a0  d4 26 c5 4c 18 f3 65 bb  a8 4c 0f 8d 6e be 7b d3  |.&.L..e..L..n.{.|
000000b0  24 9b a8 09 9c bb a3 f9  53 49 78 86 f5 24 e7 10  |$.......SIx..$..|
000000c0  ad 05 45 b8 cb 31 bd 38  b6 5c 00 02 b2 a4 62 13  |..E..1.8.\....b.|
000000d0  d5 82 6b 73 79 97 7e fa  2f 5d 3b 91 a0 21 50 9d  |..ksy.~./];..!P.|
000000e0  77 1a 32 44 e1 93 9b 9c  be bf 49 d2 f9 dc 56 23  |w.2D......I...V#|
000000f0  07 a8 ca a5 e3 e7 d1 ae  9c 22 1f 98 b1 63 b8 73  |........."...c.s|
00000100  66 3f 9f a5 6a 45 60 a7  81 eb 32 e5 42 4d 2b fd  |f?..jE`...2.BM+.|
00000110  65 6c c2 c7 74 9f 1d 6a  1c 24 32 0e 7a 94 a2 60  |el..t..j.$2.z..`|
00000120  22 77 58 c9 69 c3 55 72  e8 fb 0b 63 9d 7f 04 31  |"wX.i.Ur...c...1|
00000130  00 a2 07 76 af 95 4e 03  0a 92 10 b8 bb 1e 89 94  |...v..N.........|
00000140  45 60 01 45 bf d7 95 df  ff 2e 9e 31 0a           |E`.E.......1.|
0000014d
```

For more details on encrypting etcd data, refer to the Kubernetes documentation (*https://oreil.ly/uIylK*). There, you will find additional information on other encryption providers, how to rotate the decryption key, and the process to consider for a high-availability (HA) cluster setup.

Understanding Container Runtime Sandboxes

Containers run in a container runtime isolated from the host environment. The process or application running in the container can interact with the kernel by making syscalls. Now, we can have multiple containers (as controlled by Pods) running on a single Kubernetes cluster node and therefore the same kernel. Under certain conditions, vulnerabilities can lead to a situation where a process running a container can "break out" of its isolated environment and access another container running on the same host machine. A *container runtime sandbox* runs side-by-side with the regular container runtime but adds an additional layer of security by tightening process isolation.

There are a couple of use cases where using a container runtime sandbox may make sense. For example, your Kubernetes cluster handles the workload of different customers with the same infrastructure, a so-called multi-tenant environment. Another reason for wanting to rely on stronger container isolation is that you may not trust the process or application running in a container image, as should be the case if you pulled the container image from a public registry and you can't verify the creator or its runtime behavior.

Scenario: An Attacker Gains Access to Another Container

In this scenario, we are confronted with a developer that pulls a container image from a public registry, as referenced by a Pod. The container has not been scanned for security vulnerabilities. An attacker can push a new tag of the container image executing malicious code. After instantiating a container from the image, the malicious code running in the kernel group of container 1 can access the process running in container 2. As you can see in Figure 5-4, both containers use the same kernel of the host system.

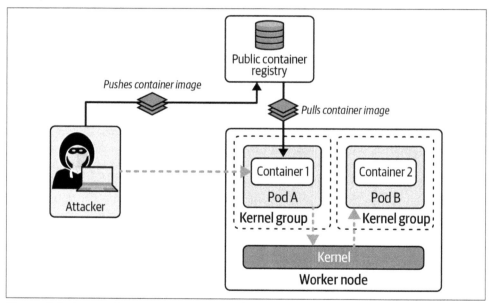

Figure 5-4. An attacker gains access to another container

Generally speaking, it's not a good idea to blindly trust public container images. One way to ensure that such a container image runs with more isolation is the container runtime sandbox. The next section will introduce you to two implementations, both of which are explicitly mentioned by the curriculum.

Available Container Runtime Sandbox Implementations

In this book, we'll only want to talk about two container runtime sandbox implementations, Kata Containers (*https://katacontainers.io*) and gVisor (*https://gvisor.dev*). Kata containers achieves container isolation by running them in a lightweight virtual machine. gVisor takes a different approach. It effectively implements a Linux kernel that runs on the host system. Therefore, syscalls are not shared anymore across all containers on the host system.

A deeper discussion on the feature sets or specific use cases for those container runtime sandbox implementations goes beyond the scope of this book. We'll simply learn how to use one solution as an example, gVisor, and how to tie it into Kubernetes. Have a look at the talk "Kata Containers and gVisor: a Quantitative Comparison" (*https://oreil.ly/PBfEn*) for an in-depth comparison.

Installing and Configuring gVisor

The following instructions (*https://oreil.ly/MlSET*) describe the steps required to install gVisor on Linux using the `apt` package manager. You will want to repeat those steps on all host machines declared as worker nodes. For the exam, you will not be expected to install gVisor or Kata Containers. You can assume that the container runtime sandbox has already been installed and configured.

Start by installing the dependencies for gVisor with the following command:

```
$ sudo apt-get update && \
  sudo apt-get install -y \
    apt-transport-https \
    ca-certificates \
    curl \
    gnupg
```

Next, configure the key used to sign archives and the repository. As you can see in the following commands, gVisor is hosted on Google storage:

```
$ curl -fsSL https://gvisor.dev/archive.key | sudo gpg --dearmor -o /usr/share/\
keyrings/gvisor-archive-keyring.gpg
$ echo "deb [arch=$(dpkg --print-architecture) signed-by=/usr/share/keyrings/\
gvisor-archive-keyring.gpg] https://storage.googleapis.com/gvisor/releases \
release main" | sudo tee /etc/apt/sources.list.d/gvisor.list > /dev/null
```

gVisor includes an Open Container Initiative (OCI) runtime called runsc. The runsc runtime integrates with tools like Docker and Kubernetes to run container runtime sandboxes. The following command installs the executable from the repository:

```
$ sudo apt-get update && sudo apt-get install -y runsc
```

Let's assume we are using containerd as the container runtime. You need to add some configuration to containerd to make it aware of runsc. You can find similar instructions for other container runtimes in the gVisor documentation:

```
$ cat <<EOF | sudo tee /etc/containerd/config.toml
version = 2
[plugins."io.containerd.runtime.v1.linux"]
  shim_debug = true
[plugins."io.containerd.grpc.v1.cri".containerd.runtimes.runc]
  runtime_type = "io.containerd.runc.v2"
[plugins."io.containerd.grpc.v1.cri".containerd.runtimes.runsc]
  runtime_type = "io.containerd.runsc.v1"
EOF
```

Finally, restart containerd to let the changes take effect:

```
$ sudo systemctl restart containerd
```

We successfully installed gVisor and can now configure Pods to use it.

Creating and Using a Runtime Class

It's a two-step approach to use a container runtime sandbox in a Pod. First, you need to create a runtime class. A RuntimeClass is a Kubernetes API resource that defines the configuration of the container runtime. Example 5-13 shows a YAML manifest of a container runtime that points to runsc as the handler we set in the containerd configuration file earlier.

Example 5-13. YAML manifest for defining a runtime class using runsc handler

```
apiVersion: node.k8s.io/v1
kind: RuntimeClass
metadata:
  name: gvisor
handler: runsc
```

We can now reference the runtime class name, gvisor, in the configuration of a Pod. Example 5-14 shows a Pod definition that assigns the runtime class using the attribute spec.runtimeClassName.

Example 5-14. YAML manifest for a Pod using a runtime class

```
apiVersion: v1
kind: Pod
metadata:
  name: nginx
spec:
  runtimeClassName: gvisor
  containers:
```

```
  - name: nginx
    image: nginx:1.23.2
```

Create the runtime class and Pod object using the apply command:

```
$ kubectl apply -f runtimeclass.yaml
runtimeclass.node.k8s.io/gvisor created
$ kubectl apply -f pod.yaml
pod/nginx created
```

You can verify that the container is running with the container runtime sandbox. Simply execute the dmesg command to examine the kernel ring buffer. The output from the command should mention gVisor, as shown in the following:

```
$ kubectl exec nginx -- dmesg
[    0.000000] Starting gVisor...
[    0.123202] Preparing for the zombie uprising...
[    0.415862] Rewriting operating system in Javascript...
[    0.593368] Reading process obituaries...
[    0.741642] Segmenting fault lines...
[    0.797360] Daemonizing children...
[    0.831010] Creating bureaucratic processes...
[    1.313731] Searching for needles in stacks...
[    1.455084] Constructing home...
[    1.834278] Gathering forks...
[    1.928142] Mounting deweydecimalfs...
[    2.109973] Setting up VFS...
[    2.157224] Ready!
```

Understanding Pod-to-Pod Encryption with mTLS

In "Using Network Policies to Restrict Pod-to-Pod Communication" on page 11, we talked about Pod-to-Pod communication. One of the big takeaways was that every Pod can talk to any other Pod by targeting its virtual IP address unless you put a more restrictive network policy in place. The communication between two Pods is unencrypted by default.

TLS provides encryption for network communication, often in conjunction with the HTTP protocol. That's when we talk about using the HTTPS protocol for calls to web pages from the browser. As part of the authentication process, the client offers its client certificate to the server for proving its identity. The server does not authenticate the client, though.

When loading a web page, the identity of the client, in this case the browser, usually doesn't matter. The important part is that the web page proves its identity. Mutual TLS (mTLS) is like TLS, but both sides have to authenticate. This approach has the following benefits. First, you achieve secure communication through encryption. Second, you can verify the client identity. An attacker cannot easily impersonate another Pod.

Scenario: An Attacker Listens to the Communication Between Two Pods

An attacker can use the default, unencrypted Pod-to-Pod network communication behavior to their advantage. As you can see in Figure 5-5, an attacker doesn't even need to break into a Pod. They can simply listen to the Pod-to-Pod communication by impersonating the sending or the receiving side, extract sensitive information, and then use it for more advanced attack vectors.

Figure 5-5. An attacker listens to Pod-to-Pod communication

You can mitigate the situation by setting up mTLS. The next section will briefly touch on the options for making that happen.

Adopting mTLS in Kubernetes

The tricky part about implementing mTLS in a Kubernetes cluster is the management of certificates. As you can imagine, we'll have to deal with a lot of certificates when implementing a microservices architecture. Those certificates are usually generated by an official certificate authority (CA) to ensure that they can be trusted. Requesting a certificate involves sending a certificate signing request (CSR) to the CA. If the CA approves the request, it creates the certificate, then signs and returns it. It's recommended to assign short lifespans to a certificate before it needs to be re-issued again. That process is called certificate rotation.

It's somewhat unclear to what degree of detail the CKS exam requires you to understand mTLS. The general process of requesting and approving a certificate is described in the Kubernetes documentation (*https://oreil.ly/QvtEQ*).

In most cases, Kubernetes administrators rely on a Kubernetes service mesh to implement mTLS instead of implementing it manually. A Kubernetes service mesh, such as Linkerd or Istio, is a tool for adding cross-cutting functionality to your cluster, like observability and security.

Another option is to use transparent encryption to ensure that traffic doesn't go on the wire unencrypted. Some of the popular CNI plugins, such as Calico (*https://oreil.ly/XZSpx*) and Cilium (*https://oreil.ly/Qsqq_*), have added support for Wire-Guard (*https://www.wireguard.com*). WireGuard is an open source, lightweight, and secure Virtual Private Network (VPN) solution that doesn't require the configuration or management of encryption keys or certificates. Many teams prefer WireGuard over a service mesh as it is easier to manage.

Services meshes and WireGuard are out of scope for the exam.

Summary

It's important to enforce security best practices for Pods. In this chapter, we reviewed different options. We looked at security contexts and how they can be defined on the Pod and container level. For example, we can configure a security context for a container to run with a non-root user and prevent the use of privileged mode. It's usually the responsibility of a developer to define those settings. The Pod Security Admission is a Kubernetes feature that takes Pod security settings one step further. You can centrally configure a Pod such that it needs to adhere to certain security standards. The configured security standard can either be enforced, audited, or just logged to standard output. Gatekeeper is an open source project that implements the functionality of the Open Policy Agent for Kubernetes. Not only can you govern the configuration for Pod objects, you can also apply policies to other kinds of objects during creation time.

Key-value pairs defined by Secrets are stored in etcd in plain text. You should configure encryption for etcd to ensure that attackers cannot read sensitive data from it. To enable encryption, create a YAML manifest for an EncryptionConfiguration, which you would then pass to the API server process with the command line option `--encryption-provider-config`.

Container runtime sandboxes help with isolating processes and applications to a stronger degree than the regular container runtime. The projects Kata Containers and gVisor are implementations of such a container runtime sandbox and can be installed and configured to work with Kubernetes. We tried gVisor. After installing and configuring gVisor, you will need to create a RuntimeClass object that points to runsc. In the Pod configuration, point to the RuntimeClass object by name.

Pod-to-Pod communication is unencrypted and unauthenticated by default. Mutual TLS makes the process more secure. Pods communicating with one another need to provide certificates to prove their identity. Implementing mTLS for a cluster with hundreds of microservices is a tedious task. Each Pod running a microservice needs to employ an approved certificate from a Client Authority. Services meshes help with adding mTLS as a feature to a Kubernetes cluster.

Exam Essentials

Practice the use of core Kubernetes features and external tools to govern security settings.
In the course of this chapter, we looked at OS-level security settings and how to govern them with different core features and external tooling. You need to understand the different options, their benefits and limitations, and be able to apply them to implement contextual requirements. Practice the use of security contexts, Pod Security Admission, and Open Policy Agent Gatekeeper. The Kubernetes ecosystem offers more tooling in this space. Feel free to explore those on your own to expand your horizon.

Understand how etcd manages Secrets data.
The CKA exam already covers the workflow of creating and using Secrets to inject sensitive configuration data into Pods. I am assuming that you already know how to do this. Every Secret key-value pair is stored in etcd. Expand your knowledge of Secret management by learning how to encrypt etcd so that an attacker with access to a host running etcd isn't able to read information in plain text.

Know how to configure the use of a container runtime sandbox.
Container runtime sandboxes help with adding stricter isolation to containers. You will not be expected to install a container runtime sandbox, such as Kata Containers or gVisor. You do need to understand the process for configuring a container runtime sandbox with the help of a RuntimeClass object and how to assign the RuntimeClass to a Pod by name.

Gain awareness of mTLS.
Setting up mTLS for all microservices running in a Pod can be extremely tedious due to certificate management. For the exam, understand the general use case for wanting to set up mTLS for Pod-to-Pod communication. You are likely not expected to actually implement it manually, though. Production Kubernetes clusters use services meshes to provide mTLS as a feature.

Sample Exercises

Solutions to these exercises are available in the Appendix.

1. Create a Pod named busybox-security-context with the container image busybox:1.28 that runs the command sh -c sleep 1h. Add a Volume of type emptydir and mount it to the path /data/test. Configure a security context with the following attributes: runAsUser: 1000, runAsGroup: 3000, and fsGroup: 2000. Furthermore, set the attribute allowPrivilegeEscalation to false.

Shell into the container, navigate to the directory /data/test, and create the file named hello.txt. Check the group assigned to the file. What's the value? Exit out of the container.

2. Create a Pod Security Admission (PSA) rule. In the namespace called audited, create a Pod Security Standard (PSS) with the level baseline that should be rendered to the console.

   Try to create a Pod in the namespace that violates the PSS and produces a message on the console log. You can provide any name, container image, and security configuration you like. Will the Pod be created? What PSA level needs to be configured to prevent the creation of the Pod?

3. Install Gatekeeper on your cluster. Create a Gatekeeper ConstraintTemplate object that defines the minimum and maximum number of replicas controlled by a ReplicaSet. Instantiate a Constraint object that uses the ConstraintTemplate. Set the minimum number of replicas to 3 and the maximum number to 10.

   Create a Deployment object that sets the number of replicas to 15. Gatekeeper should not allow the Deployment, ReplicaSet, and Pods to be created. An error message should be rendered. Try again to create the Deployment object but with a replica number of 7. Verify that all objects have been created successfully.

4. Configure encryption for etcd using the aescbc provider. Create a new Secret object of type Opaque. Provide the key-value pair api-key=YZvkiWUkycv spyGHk3fQRAkt. Query for the value of the Secret using etcdctl. What's the encrypted value?

5. Navigate to the directory *app-a/ch05/gvisor* of the checked-out GitHub repository *bmuschko/cks-study-guide* (*https://oreil.ly/sImXZ*). Start up the VMs running the cluster using the command vagrant up. The cluster consists of a single control plane node named kube-control-plane and one worker node named kube-worker-1. Once done, shut down the cluster using vagrant destroy -f.

   gVisor has been installed in the VM kube-worker-1. Shell into the VM and create a RuntimeClass object named container-runtime-sandbox with runsc as the handler. Then create a Pod with the name nginx and the container image nginx:1.23.2 and assign the RuntimeClass to it.

   Prerequisite: This exercise requires the installation of the tools Vagrant (*https://oreil.ly/FiyeH*) and VirtualBox (*https://oreil.ly/WW8IK*).

CHAPTER 6

Supply Chain Security

Earlier chapters primarily focused on securing the Kubernetes cluster and its components, the OS infrastructure used to run cluster nodes, and the operational aspects for running workload on a cluster node with existing container images. This chapter takes a step back and drills into the process, best practices, and tooling for designing, building, and optimizing container images.

Sometimes, you do not want to create your own container image but instead consume an existing one produced by a different team or company. Scanning container images for known vulnerabilities in a manual or automated fashion should be part of your vetting process before using them to run your workload. We'll talk through some options relevant to the CKS exam used to identify, analyze, and mitigate security risks for pre-built container images.

At a high level, this chapter covers the following concepts:

- Minimizing base image footprint
- Securing the supply chain
- Using static analysis of user workload
- Scanning images for known vulnerabilities

Minimizing the Base Image Footprint

The process for building a container image looks straightforward on the surface level; however, the devil is often in the details. It may not be obvious to someone new to the topic to refrain from building a container image that is unnecessarily too large in size, riddled with vulnerabilities, and not optimized for container layer caching. We'll address all of those aspects in the course of this chapter with the help of the container engine Docker.

Scenario: An Attacker Exploits Container Vulnerabilities

One of the first decisions you have to make when defining a Dockerfile is the selection of a base image. The base image provides the operating system and additional dependencies, and it may expose shell access.

Some of the base images you can choose from on a public registry like Docker Hub are large in size and will likely contain functionality you don't necessarily need to run your application inside of it. The operating system itself, as well as any dependencies available with the base image, can expose vulnerabilities.

In Figure 6-1, the attacker was able to figure out details about the container by gaining access to it. Those vulnerabilities can now be used as a launching pad for more advanced attacks.

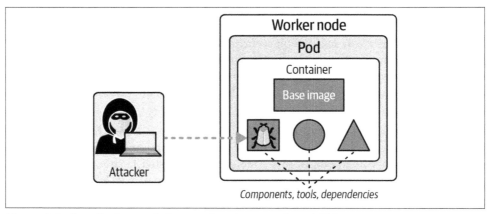

Figure 6-1. An attacker exploits container image vulnerabilities

It is recommended to use a base image with a minimal set of functionality and dependencies. The next couple of sections will explain the methods for creating a more optimized base image that's faster to build, quicker to download from a container registry, and that will ultimately lead to a smaller attack surface simply by reducing the bloat. The next sections will touch on the most important techniques. You can find a more detailed list of best practices for writing Dockerfiles in the Docker documentation (*https://oreil.ly/43Diy*).

Picking a Base Image Small in Size

Some container images can have a size of a gigabyte or even more. Do you really need all the functionality bundled with such a container image? Unlikely. Thankfully, many container producers upload a wide range of variations of their container images for the same release. One of those variations is an `alpine` image, a small, lightweight, and less vulnerable Linux distribution. As you can see in the following output, the downloaded `alpine` container image with the tag `3.17.0` only has a size of 7.05MB:

```
$ docker pull alpine:3.17.0
...
$ docker image ls alpine
REPOSITORY    TAG       IMAGE ID       CREATED       SIZE
alpine        3.17.0    49176f190c7e   3 weeks ago   7.05MB
```

The `alpine` container image comes with an `sh` shell you can use to troubleshoot the process running inside of the container. You can use the following command to open an interactive shell in a new container:

```
$ docker run -it alpine:3.17.0 /bin/sh
/ # exit
```

While runtime troubleshooting functionality can be useful, offering a shell as part of a container image increases the size of it and potentially opens the door for attackers. Additionally, the more software there is inside of a container image, the more vulnerabilities it will have.

You can further reduce the container image size and the attack surface by using a distroless image (*https://oreil.ly/J6Vra*) offered by Google. The following command downloads the latest tag of the container image `gcr.io/distroless/static-debian11` and renders its details. The size of the container image is only 2.34MB:

```
$ docker pull gcr.io/distroless/static-debian11
...
$ docker image ls gcr.io/distroless/static-debian11:latest
REPOSITORY                          TAG      IMAGE ID       CREATED        \
  SIZE
gcr.io/distroless/static-debian11   latest   901590160d4d   53 years ago   \
  2.34MB
```

A distroless container image does not ship with any shell, which you can observe by running the following command:

```
$ docker run -it gcr.io/distroless/static-debian11:latest /bin/sh
docker: Error response from daemon: failed to create shim task: OCI runtime \
create failed: runc create failed: unable to start container process: exec: \
"/bin/sh": stat /bin/sh: no such file or directory: unknown.
```

Kubernetes offers the concept of ephemeral containers for troubleshooting distroless containers. Those containers are meant to be disposable and can be deployed for troubleshooting minimal containers that would usually not allow opening a shell. Discussing ephemeral containers is out of scope of this book, but you can find more information about them in the Kubernetes documentation (*https://oreil.ly/IRjP3*).

Using a Multi-Stage Approach for Building Container Images

As a developer, you can decide to build the application code as part of the instructions in a Dockerfile. This process may include compiling the code and building a binary that should become the entry point of the container image. Having all the necessarily tools and dependencies available to implement the process will automatically blow up the size of the container image, plus you won't need those dependencies at runtime anymore.

The idea of a multi-stage build in Docker (*https://oreil.ly/znQc3*) is that you separate the build stage from the runtime stage. As a result, all dependencies needed in the build stage will be discarded after the process has been performed and therefore do not end up in the final container image. This approach leads to a much smaller container image size by removing all the unnecessary cruft.

While we won't go into the details of crafting and fully understanding multi-stage Dockerfile, I want to show you the differences on a high level. We'll start by showing you a Dockerfile that builds and tests a simple program using the programming language Go, as shown in Example 6-1. In essence, we are using a base image (*https://oreil.ly/nwLtT*) that includes Go 1.19.4. The Go runtime provides the go executes, which we'll invoke to execute the tests and build the binary of the application.

Example 6-1. Building and testing a Go program using a Go base image

```
FROM golang:1.19.4-alpine ❶
WORKDIR /app

COPY go.mod .
COPY go.sum .
RUN go mod download

COPY . .
RUN CGO_ENABLED=0 go test -v ❷
RUN go build -o /go-sample-app . ❸
CMD ["/go-sample-app"]
```

❶ Uses a Go base image

❷ Executes the tests against the application code

❸ Builds the binary of the Go application

You can produce the image using the docker build command, as shown in the following:

```
$ docker build . -t go-sample-app:0.0.1
...
```

The size of the result container image is pretty big, 348MB, and there's a good reason for it. It includes the Go runtime, even though we don't actually need it anymore when starting the container. The go build command produced the binary that we can run as the container's entry point:

```
$ docker images
REPOSITORY       TAG      IMAGE ID       CREATED          SIZE
go-sample-app    0.0.1    88175f3ab0d3   44 seconds ago   358MB
```

Next up, we'll have a look at the multi-stage approach. In a multi-stage Dockerfile, you define at least two stages. In Example 6-2, we specify a stage aliased with build to run the tests and build the binary, similarly to what we've done earlier. A second stage copies the binary produced by the stage build into a dedicated directory; however, it uses the alpine base image to run it. When running the docker build command, the stage build will not be included in the final container image anymore.

Example 6-2. Building and testing a Go program as part of a multi-stage Dockerfile

```
FROM golang:1.19.4-alpine AS build  ❶
RUN apk add --no-cache git
WORKDIR /tmp/go-sample-app
COPY go.mod .
COPY go.sum .
RUN go mod download
COPY . .

RUN CGO_ENABLED=0 go test -v  ❷
RUN go build -o ./out/go-sample-app .  ❸

FROM alpine:3.17.0  ❹
RUN apk add ca-certificates
COPY --from=build /tmp/go-sample-app/out/go-sample-app /app/go-sample-app  ❺
CMD ["/app/go-sample-app"]
```

❶ Uses a Go base image for building and testing the program in the stage named build.

❷ Executes the tests against the application code.

❸ Builds the binary of the Go application.

❹ Uses a much smaller base image for running the application in a container.

❺ Copies the application binary produced in the build stage and uses it as the command to run when the container is started.

The resulting container image size is significantly smaller when using the `alpine` base image, only 12MB. You can verify the outcome by running the `docker build` command again and inspecting the size of the container image by listing it:

```
$ docker build . -t go-sample-app:0.0.1
...
$ docker images
REPOSITORY      TAG     IMAGE ID       CREATED         SIZE
go-sample-app   0.0.1   88175f3ab0d3   44 seconds ago  12MB
```

Not only did we reduce the size, we also reduced the attack surface by including fewer dependencies. You can further reduce the size of the container image by incorporating a distroless base image instead of the `alpine` base image.

Reducing the Number of Layers

Every Dockerfile consists of an ordered list of instructions. Only some instructions create a read-only layer in the resulting container image. Those instructions are FROM, COPY, RUN, and CMD. All other instructions will not create a layer as they create temporary intermediate images. The more layers you add to the container image, the slower will be the build execution time and/or the bigger will be the size of the container image. Therefore, you need to be cautious about the instructions used in your Dockerfile to minimize the footprint of the container image.

It's common practice to execute multiple commands in a row. You may define those commands using a list of RUN instructions on individual lines, as shown in Example 6-3.

Example 6-3. A Dockerfile specifying multiple RUN instructions

```
FROM ubuntu:22.10
RUN apt-get update -y
RUN apt-get upgrade -y
RUN apt-get install -y curl
```

Each RUN instruction will create a layer, potentially adding to the size of the container image. It's more efficient to string them together with && to ensure that only a single layer will be produced. Example 6-4 shows an example of this optimization technique.

Example 6-4. A Dockerfile specifying multiple RUN instructions

```
FROM ubuntu:22.10
RUN apt-get update -y && apt-get upgrade -y && apt-get install -y curl
```

Using Container Image Optimization Tools

It's easy to forget about the optimization practices mentioned previously. The open source community developed a couple of tools that can help with inspecting a produced container image. Their functionalities provide useful tips for pairing down on unnecessary layers, files, and folders:

DockerSlim

> DockerSlim will optimize and secure your container image by analyzing your application and its dependencies. You can find more information in the tool's GitHub repository (*https://oreil.ly/ZbeZl*).

Dive

> Dive is a tool for exploring the layers baked into a container image. It makes it easy to identify unnecessary layers, which you can further optimize on. The code and documentation for Dive are available in a GitHub repository (*https://oreil.ly/UBqqj*).

This is only the short list of container image optimization tools. In "Static Analysis of Workload" on page 130, we'll have a look at other tools that focus on the static analysis of Dockerfiles and Kubernetes manifests.

Securing the Supply Chain

A supply chain automates the process of producing a container image and operating it in a runtime environment, in this case Kubernetes. We already touched on a couple of tools that can be integrated into the supply chain to support the aspect of container image optimization. In this section, we'll expand on practices that target security aspects. Refer to the book *Container Security* by Liz Rice (O'Reilly) to learn more.

Signing Container Images

You can sign a container image before pushing it to a container registry. Signing can be achieved with the `docker trust sign` command, which adds a signature to the container image, the so-called image digest. An image digest is derived from the contents of the container image and commonly represented in the form of SHA256. When consuming the container image, Kubernetes can compare the image digest with the contents of the image to ensure that it hasn't been tampered with.

Scenario: An Attacker Injects Malicious Code into a Container Image

The Kubernetes component that verifies the image digest is the kubelet. If you configured the image pull policy (*https://oreil.ly/0wSjy*) to `Always`, the kubelet will query for the image digest from the container registry even though it may have downloaded and verified the container image before.

An attacker can try to modify the contents of an existing container image, inject malicious code, and upload it to the container registry with the same tag, as shown in Figure 6-2. The malicious code running in the container could then send sensitive information to a third-party server accessible by the attacker.

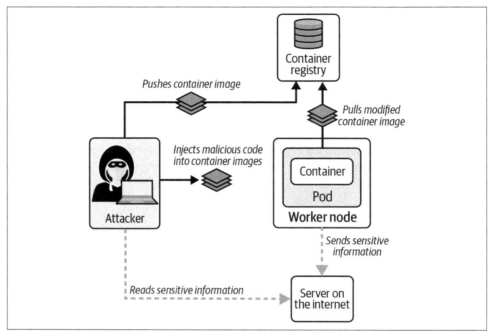

Figure 6-2. An attacker injects malicious code into a container image

Image checksum validation is not automatic

Image digest validation is an opt-in functionality in Kubernetes. When defining Pods, make sure you spell out the image digest explicitly for all container images.

Validating Container Images

In Kubernetes, you're able to append the SHA256 image digest to the specification of a container. For example, this can be achieved with the attribute `spec.contain ers[].image`. The image digest is generally available in the container registry. For example, Figure 6-3 shows the image digest for the container image `alpine:3.17.0` on Docker Hub (*https://oreil.ly/ZAV_H*). In this example, the image digest is `sha256:c0d488a800e4127c334ad20d61d7bc21b4097540327217dfab52262adc02380c`.

Figure 6-3. The image digest of the `alpine:3.17.0` container image on Docker Hub

Let's see the image digest in action. Instead of using the tag, Example 6-5 specifies the container image by appending the image digest.

Example 6-5. A Pod using a valid container image digest

```
apiVersion: v1
kind: Pod
metadata:
  name: alpine-valid
spec:
  containers:
  - name: alpine
    image: alpine@sha256:c0d488a800e4127c334ad20d61d7bc21b40 \
            97540327217dfab52262adc02380c
    command: ["/bin/sh"]
    args: ["-c", "while true; do echo hello; sleep 10; done"]
```

Creating the Pod will work as expected. The image digest will be verified and the container transitions into the "Running" status:

```
$ kubectl apply -f pod-valid-image-digest.yaml
pod/alpine-valid created
$ kubectl get pod alpine-valid
NAME           READY   STATUS    RESTARTS   AGE
alpine-valid   1/1     Running   0          6s
```

Example 6-6 shows the same Pod definition; however, the image digest has been changed so that it does not match with the contents of the container image.

Example 6-6. A Pod using an invalid container image digest

```
apiVersion: v1
kind: Pod
metadata:
  name: alpine-invalid
spec:
  containers:
  - name: alpine
    image: alpine@sha256:d006a643bccb6e9adbabaae668533c7f2e5 \
            111572fffb5c61cb7fcba7ef4150b
```

```
command: ["/bin/sh"]
args: ["-c", "while true; do echo hello; sleep 10; done"]
```

You will see that Kubernetes can still create the Pod object but it can't properly validate the hash of the container image. This results in the status "ErrImagePull." As you can see from the event log, the container image couldn't even be pulled from the container registry:

```
$ kubectl get pods
NAME              READY   STATUS         RESTARTS   AGE
alpine-invalid    0/1     ErrImagePull   0          29s
$ kubectl describe pod alpine-invalid
...
Events:
  Type      Reason     Age    From              Message
  ----      ------     ----   ----              -------
  Normal    Scheduled  13s    default-scheduler Successfully assigned default \
  /alpine-invalid to minikube
  Normal    Pulling    13s    kubelet           Pulling image "alpine@sha256: \
  d006a643bccb6e9adbabaae668533c7f2e5111572fffb5c61cb7fcba7ef4150b"
  Warning   Failed     11s    kubelet           Failed to pull image \
  "alpine@sha256:d006a643bccb6e9adbabaae668533c7f2e5111572fffb5c61cb7fcba7ef4 \
  150b": rpc error: code = Unknown desc = Error response from daemon: manifest \
  for alpine@sha256:d006a643bccb6e9adbabaae668533c7f2e5111572fffb5c61cb7fcba7e \
  f4150b not found: manifest unknown: manifest unknown
  Warning   Failed     11s    kubelet           Error: ErrImagePull
  Normal    BackOff    11s    kubelet           Back-off pulling image \
  "alpine@sha256:d006a643bccb6e9adbabaae668533c7f2e5111572fffb5c61cb7fcba7ef415 \
  0b"
  Warning   Failed     11s    kubelet           Error: ImagePullBackOff
```

Using Public Image Registries

Whenever a Pod is created, the container runtime engine will download the declared container image from a container registry if it isn't available locally yet. This runtime behavior can be further tweaked using the image pull policy (https://oreil.ly/ZBMnH).

The prefix in the image name declares the domain name of the registry; e.g., gcr.io/google-containers/debian-base:v1.0.1 refers to the container image google-containers/debian-base:v1.0.1 in the Google Cloud container registry (https://oreil.ly/QFxfY), denoted by gcr.io. The container runtime will try to resolve it from docker.io, the Docker Hub container registry (https://hub.docker.com) if you leave off the domain name in the container image declaration.

Scenario: An Attacker Uploads a Malicious Container Image

While it is convenient to resolve container images from public container registries, it doesn't come without risks. Anyone with a login to those container registries can upload new images. Consuming container images usually doesn't even require an account.

As shown in Figure 6-4, an attacker can upload a container image containing malicious code to a public registry using stolen credentials. Any container referencing the container image from that registry will automatically run the malicious code.

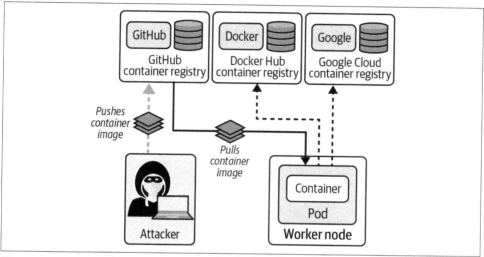

Figure 6-4. An attacker uploads a malicious container image

On an enterprise level, you need to control which container registries you trust. It's recommended to set up your own container registry within your company's network, which you can fully control and govern. Alternatively, you can set up a private container registry in a cloud provider environment, not accessible by anyone else.

One of the prominent binary repository managers you can choose from is JFrog Artifactory (*https://oreil.ly/jdF_6*). The product fully supports storing, scanning, and serving container images. Any consumer of container images should only be allowed to pull images from your whitelisted container registry. All other container registries should be denied.

Whitelisting Allowed Image Registries with OPA GateKeeper

One way to govern container registry usage is with OPA Gatekeeper. We discussed the installation process and functionality of OPA Gatekeeper in "Understanding Open Policy Agent (OPA) and Gatekeeper" on page 95. Here, we'll' touch on the constraint template and constraint for allowing trusted container registries.

Example 6-7 shows the constraint template (*https://oreil.ly/hvgnr*) I got directly from the OPA Gatekeeper library. As input properties, the constraint template defines an array of strings representing the prefixes of container registries. The Rego rules verify not only the assigned container images for the attribute `spec.containers[]` but also `spec.initContainers[]` and `spec.ephemeralContainers[]`.

Example 6-7. An OPA Gatekeeper constraint template for enforcing container registries

```yaml
apiVersion: templates.gatekeeper.sh/v1
kind: ConstraintTemplate
metadata:
  name: k8sallowedrepos
  annotations:
    metadata.gatekeeper.sh/title: "Allowed Repositories"
    metadata.gatekeeper.sh/version: 1.0.0
    description: >-
      Requires container images to begin with a string from the specified list.
spec:
  crd:
    spec:
      names:
        kind: K8sAllowedRepos
      validation:
        openAPIV3Schema:
          type: object
          properties:
            repos:
              description: The list of prefixes a container image is allowed to have.
              type: array
              items:
                type: string
  targets:
    - target: admission.k8s.gatekeeper.sh
      rego: |
        package k8sallowedrepos

        violation[{"msg": msg}] {
          container := input.review.object.spec.containers[_]
          satisfied := [good | repo = input.parameters.repos[_] ; \
          good = startswith(container.image, repo)]
          not any(satisfied)
          msg := sprintf("container <%v> has an invalid image repo <%v>, allowed \
          repos are %v", [container.name, container.image, input.parameters.repos])
        }

        violation[{"msg": msg}] {
          container := input.review.object.spec.initContainers[_]
          satisfied := [good | repo = input.parameters.repos[_] ; \
          good = startswith(container.image, repo)]
          not any(satisfied)
          msg := sprintf("initContainer <%v> has an invalid image repo <%v>, \
          allowed repos are %v", [container.name, container.image, \
          input.parameters.repos])
```

```
    }

    violation[{"msg": msg}] {
      container := input.review.object.spec.ephemeralContainers[_]
      satisfied := [good | repo = input.parameters.repos[_] ; \
      good = startswith(container.image, repo)]
      not any(satisfied)
      msg := sprintf("ephemeralContainer <%v> has an invalid image repo <%v>, \
      allowed repos are %v", [container.name, container.image, \
      input.parameters.repos])
    }
```

The constraint shown in Example 6-8 is in charge of defining which container registries we want to allow. You'd usually go with a domain name of a server hosted in your company's network. Here, we are going to use gcr.io/ for demonstration purposes.

Example 6-8. An OPA Gatekeeper constraint assigning Google Cloud registry as trusted repository

```
apiVersion: constraints.gatekeeper.sh/v1beta1
kind: K8sAllowedRepos
metadata:
  name: repo-is-gcr
spec:
  match:
    kinds:
      - apiGroups: [""]
        kinds: ["Pod"]
  parameters:
    repos:
      - "gcr.io/"
```

Let's create both objects using the apply command:

```
$ kubectl apply -f allowed-repos-constraint-template.yaml
constrainttemplate.templates.gatekeeper.sh/k8sallowedrepos created
$ kubectl apply -f gcr-allowed-repos-constraint.yaml
k8sallowedrepos.constraints.gatekeeper.sh/repo-is-gcr created
```

In the constraint, we didn't specify a namespace that the rules should apply to. Therefore, they'll apply across all namespaces in the cluster. The following commands verify that the whitelisting rules work as expected. The following command tries to create a Pod using the nginx container image from Docker Hub. The creation of the Pod is denied with an appropriate error message:

```
$ kubectl run nginx --image=nginx:1.23.3
Error from server (Forbidden): admission webhook "validation.gatekeeper.sh" \
denied the request: [repo-is-gcr] container <nginx> has an invalid image \
repo <nginx:1.23.3>, allowed repos are ["gcr.io/"]
```

The next command creates a Pod with a container image from the Google Cloud container registry. The operation is permitted and the Pod object is created:

```
$ kubectl run busybox --image=gcr.io/google-containers/busybox:1.27.2
pod/busybox created
$ kubectl get pods
NAME       READY   STATUS      RESTARTS     AGE
busybox    0/1     Completed   1 (2s ago)   3s
```

Whitelisting Allowed Image Registries with the ImagePolicyWebhook Admission Controller Plugin

Another way to validate the use of allowed image registries is to intercept a call to the API server when a Pod is about to be created. This mechanism can be achieved by enabling an admission controller plugin. Once configured, the logic of an admission controller plugin is automatically invoked when the API server receives the request, but after it could authenticate and authorize the caller. We already touched on the phases an API call has to go through in "Processing a Request" on page 44.

The admission controller provides a way to approve, deny, or mutate a request before the request takes effect. For example, we can inspect the data sent with the API request to create a Pod, iterate over the assigned container images, and execute custom logic to validate the container image notation. If the container image doesn't stick to the expected conventions, we can deny the creation of the Pod. Figure 6-5 illustrates the high-level workflow.

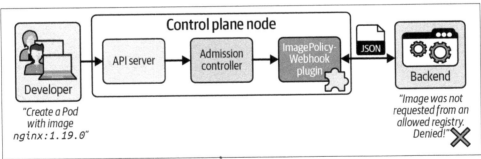

Figure 6-5. Intercepting a Pod-specific API call and handling it with a webhook

The ImagePolicyWebhook (*https://oreil.ly/JxmUu*) admission controller plugin is one of the plugins we can configure for intercepting Kubernetes API calls. You can probably derive the plugin's functionality from its name. It defines a policy for all defined container images in a Pod. To compare container images with the defined policy, the plugin calls off to a service external to Kubernetes via HTTPS, a webhook. The external service then makes the decision on how to validate the data. In the context of the admission controller plugin, the external service is also referred to as *backend*.

Implementing the Backend Application

The backend application can be implemented with a programming language of your choice. There are only three requirements it must fulfill:

1. It's a web application that can handle HTTPS requests.
2. It can accept and parse JSON request payloads.
3. It can send a JSON response payload.

Implementing the backend application is not part of the CKS exam, but you can find a sample Go-based implementation in the GitHub repository (*https://oreil.ly/OF4fF*) of this book. Be aware that the code is not considered to be production-ready.

The following commands demonstrate the runtime behavior of the application accessible at `https://localhost:8080/validate`. You can find an example request and response JSON body in the Kubernetes documentation (*https://oreil.ly/8GaQe*).

The following `curl` command calls the validation logic for the container image `nginx:1.19.0`. As you can see from the JSON response, the image is denied:

```
$ curl -X POST -H "Content-Type: application/json" -k -d \'{"apiVersion": \
"imagepolicy.k8s.io/v1alpha1", "kind": "ImageReview", "spec": \
{"containers": [{"image": "nginx:1.19.0"}]}}' https://localhost:8080/validate
{"apiVersion": "imagepolicy.k8s.io/v1alpha1", "kind": "ImageReview", \
"status": {"allowed": false, "reason": "Denied request: [container 1 \
has an invalid image repo nginx:1.19.0, allowed repos are [gcr.io/]]"}}
```

The following `curl` command calls the validation logic for the container image `gcr.io/nginx:1.19.0`. As you can see from the JSON response, the image is allowed:

```
$ curl -X POST -H "Content-Type: application/json"  -k -d '{"apiVersion": \
"imagepolicy.k8s.io/v1alpha1", "kind": "ImageReview", "spec": {"containers": \
[{"image": "gcr.io/nginx:1.19.0"}]}}' https://localhost:8080/validate
{"apiVersion": "imagepolicy.k8s.io/v1alpha1", "kind": "ImageReview", \
"status": {"allowed": true, "reason": ""}}
```

Configuring the ImagePolicyWebhook Admission Controller Plugin

For the exam, you are expected to understand how to "wire" the ImagePolicyWebhook admission controller plugin. This section will walk you through the process. First, you'll need to create a configuration file for the admission controller so it knows what plugins to use and how it should behave at runtime. Create the file `/etc/kubernetes/admission-control/image-policy-webhook-admission-config.yaml` and populate it with the content shown in Example 6-9.

Example 6-9. The admission controller configuration file

```
apiVersion: apiserver.config.k8s.io/v1
kind: AdmissionConfiguration
plugins:
  - name: ImagePolicyWebhook ❶
    configuration:
      imagePolicy:
        kubeConfigFile: /etc/kubernetes/admission-control/ \
                        imagepolicywebhook.kubeconfig ❷
        allowTTL: 50
        denyTTL: 50
        retryBackoff: 500
        defaultAllow: false ❸
```

❶ Provides the configuration for the ImagePolicyWebhook plugin.

❷ Points to the configuration file used to configure the backend.

❸ Denies an API request if the backend cannot be reached. The default is true but setting it to false is far more sensible.

Next, create the file referenced by the `plugins[].configuration.imagePolicy.kube ConfigFile` attribute. The contents of the file point to the HTTPS URL of the external service. It also defines the client certificate and key file, as well as the CA file on disk. Example 6-10 shows the contents of the configuration file.

Example 6-10. The image policy configuration file

```
apiVersion: v1
kind: Config
preferences: {}
clusters:
  - name: image-validation-webhook
    cluster:
      certificate-authority: /etc/kubernetes/admission-control/ca.crt
      server: https://image-validation-webhook:8080/validate ❶
contexts:
- context:
    cluster: image-validation-webhook
    user: api-server-client
  name: image-validation-webhook
current-context: image-validation-webhook
users:
  - name: api-server-client
    user:
      client-certificate: /etc/kubernetes/admission-control/api-server-client.crt
      client-key: /etc/kubernetes/admission-control/api-server-client.key
```

❶ The URL to the backend service. Must use the HTTPS protocol.

Enable the ImagePolicyWebhook admission controller plugin for the API server and point the admission controller to the configuration file. To achieve this, edit the configuration file of the API server, usually found at /etc/kubernetes/manifests/kube-apiserver.yaml.

Find the command line option --enable-admission-plugins and append the value ImagePolicyWebhook to the existing list of plugins, separated by a comma. Provide the command line option --admission-control-config-file if it doesn't exist yet, and set the value to /etc/kubernetes/admission-control/image-policy-webhook-admission-configuration.yaml. Given that the configuration file lives in a new directory, you will have to define it as a Volume and mount it to the container. Example 6-11 shows the relevant options for the API server container.

Example 6-11. The API server configuration file

```
...
spec:
  containers:
  - command:
    - kube-apiserver
    - --enable-admission-plugins=NodeRestriction,ImagePolicyWebhook
    - --admission-control-config-file=/etc/kubernetes/admission-control/ \
      image-policy-webhook-admission-configuration.yaml
    ...
    volumeMounts:
    ...
    - name: admission-control
      mountPath: /etc/kubernetes/admission-control
      readonly: true
  volumes:
  ...
  - name: admission-control
    hostPath:
      path: /etc/kubernetes/admission-control
      type: DirectoryOrCreate
...
```

The Pod running the API server should automatically restart. This process may take a couple of minutes. Restart the kubelet service with the command sudo systemctl restart kubelet should the API server not come up by itself. Once fully restarted, you should be able to query for it:

```
$ kubectl get pods -n kube-system
NAME                            READY   STATUS    RESTARTS   AGE
...
kube-apiserver-control-plane    1/1     Running   0          69s
```

Any API call that requests the creation of a Pod will now be routed to the backend. Based on the validation result, the creation of the object will be allowed or denied.

Static Analysis of Workload

Throughout this book, we talk about best practices for Dockerfiles and Kubernetes manifests. You can inspect those files manually, find undesired configurations, and fix them by hand. This approach requires a lot of intricate knowledge and is very tedious and error-prone. It is much more convenient and efficient to analyze workload files in an automated fashion with proper tooling. The list of commercial and open source tooling for static analysis is long. In this section, we are going to present the functionality of two options, Haskell Dockerfile Linter and Kubesec.

On an enterprise level, where you have to process hundreds or even thousands of workload files, you'd do so with the help of a continuous delivery pipeline, as shown in Figure 6-6.

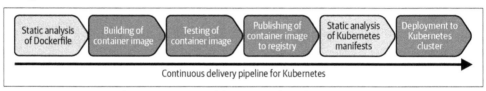

Figure 6-6. An exemplary continuous delivery pipeline for Kubernetes

Relevant static analysis tools can be invoked as a quality gate at an early stage of the pipeline even before a container image is built, pushed to a registry, or deployed to a Kubernetes cluster. For a deep dive on the principles and practices of continuous delivery, see the excellent book *Continuous Delivery* by Jez Humble and David Farley (Addison-Wesley Professional).

Using Hadolint for Analyzing Dockerfiles

Haskell Dockerfile Linter (*https://oreil.ly/C9bvu*), also called hadolint in short, is a linter for Dockerfiles. The tool inspects a Dockerfile based on best practices (*https://oreil.ly/Fwksr*) listed on the Docker documentation page. Example 6-12 shows an unoptimized Dockerfile for building a container image running a Go-based application.

Example 6-12. An unoptimized Dockerfile

```
FROM golang
COPY main.go .
RUN go build main.go
CMD ["./main"]
```

The Haskell Dockerfile Linter supports a mode of operation that lets you point the `hadolint` executable to a Dockerfile on disk. You can see the command execution that follows, including the discovered warning messages produced by the analysis:

```
$ hadolint Dockerfile
Dockerfile:1 DL3006 warning: Always tag the version of an image explicitly
Dockerfile:2 DL3045 warning: `COPY` to a relative destination without \
`WORKDIR` set.
```

The output of the command suggests that you should assign a tag to the base image. The existing Dockerfile will pull the `latest` tag, which will resolve to the newest Go container image. This practice can result in an incompatibility between the Go runtime version and the application code. Defining a working directory for copying resources helps with keeping operating system-specific directories and files separate from application-specific directories and files. Example 6-13 fixes the warning messages found by the Haskell Dockerfile Linter.

Example 6-13. An optimized Dockerfile

```
FROM golang:1.19.4-alpine
WORKDIR /app
COPY main.go .
RUN go build main.go
CMD ["./main"]
```

Another execution against the modified Dockerfile leads to a successful exit code, and no additional warning messages will be rendered:

```
$ hadolint Dockerfile
```

The Dockerfile now follows best practices, as perceived by hadolint.

Using Kubesec for Analyzing Kubernetes Manifests

Kubesec (*https://kubesec.io*) is a tool for analyzing Kubernetes manifests. It can be executed as a binary, Docker container, admission controller plugin, and even as a plugin for `kubectl`. To demonstrate its use, we'll set up a YAML manifest file `pod-initial-kubesec-test.yaml`, shown in Example 6-14 as a starting point.

Example 6-14. A Pod YAML manifest using initial security settings

```
apiVersion: v1
kind: Pod
metadata:
  name: kubesec-demo
spec:
  containers:
  - name: kubesec-demo
```

```
image: gcr.io/google-samples/node-hello:1.0
securityContext:
  readOnlyRootFilesystem: true
```

Upon inspecting the Pod configuration, you may already have some suggestions on what could be improved based on the content of the previous chapters. Let's see what Kubesec is going to recommend.

The simplest way to invoke Kubesec is to run the logic in a container with the help of Docker. The following command feeds the contents of the YAML manifest to the standard input stream. The result, formatted in JSON, renders a score, provides a human-readable message of the outcome, and advises on changes to be made:

```
$ docker run -i kubesec/kubesec:512c5e0 scan /dev/stdin \
  < pod-initial-kubesec-test.yaml
[
  {
    "object": "Pod/kubesec-demo.default",
    "valid": true,
    "message": "Passed with a score of 1 points",
    "score": 1,
    "scoring": {
      "advise": [
        {
          "selector": ".spec .serviceAccountName",
          "reason": "Service accounts restrict Kubernetes API access and \
                     should be configured with least privilege"
        },
        {
          "selector": ".metadata .annotations .\"container.apparmor.security. \
                       beta.kubernetes.io/nginx\"",
          "reason": "Well defined AppArmor policies may provide greater \
                     protection from unknown threats. WARNING: NOT PRODUCTION \
                     READY"
        },
        {
          "selector": "containers[] .resources .requests .cpu",
          "reason": "Enforcing CPU requests aids a fair balancing of \
                     resources across the cluster"
        },
        {
          "selector": ".metadata .annotations .\"container.seccomp.security. \
                       alpha.kubernetes.io/pod\"",
          "reason": "Seccomp profiles set minimum privilege and secure against \
                     unknown threats"
        },
        {
          "selector": "containers[] .resources .limits .memory",
          "reason": "Enforcing memory limits prevents DOS via resource \
                     exhaustion"
        },
        {
```

```
      "selector": "containers[] .resources .limits .cpu",
      "reason": "Enforcing CPU limits prevents DOS via resource exhaustion"
    },
    {
      "selector": "containers[] .securityContext .runAsNonRoot == true",
      "reason": "Force the running image to run as a non-root user to \
                 ensure least privilege"
    },
    {
      "selector": "containers[] .resources .requests .memory",
      "reason": "Enforcing memory requests aids a fair balancing of \
                 resources across the cluster"
    },
    {
      "selector": "containers[] .securityContext .capabilities .drop",
      "reason": "Reducing kernel capabilities available to a container \
                 limits its attack surface"
    },
    {
      "selector": "containers[] .securityContext .runAsUser -gt 10000",
      "reason": "Run as a high-UID user to avoid conflicts with the \
                 host's user table"
    },
    {
      "selector": "containers[] .securityContext .capabilities .drop | \
                   index(\"ALL\")",
      "reason": "Drop all capabilities and add only those required to \
                 reduce syscall attack surface"
    }
  ]
}
}
]
```

A touched-up version of the original YAML manifest can be found in Example 6-15. Here, we incorporated some of the recommended changes proposed by Kubesec.

Example 6-15. A Pod YAML manifest using improved security settings

```
apiVersion: v1
kind: Pod
metadata:
  name: kubesec-demo
spec:
  containers:
  - name: kubesec-demo
    image: gcr.io/google-samples/node-hello:1.0
    resources:
      requests:
        memory: "64Mi"
        cpu: "250m"
      limits:
```

```
      memory: "128Mi"
      cpu: "500m"
securityContext:
  readOnlyRootFilesystem: true
  runAsNonRoot: true
  runAsUser: 20000
  capabilities:
    drop: ["ALL"]
```

Executing the same Docker command against the changed Pod YAML manifest will render an improved score and reduce the number of advised messages:

```
$ docker run -i kubesec/kubesec:512c5e0 scan /dev/stdin \
  < pod-improved-kubesec-test.yaml
[
  {
    "object": "Pod/kubesec-demo.default",
    "valid": true,
    "message": "Passed with a score of 9 points",
    "score": 9,
    "scoring": {
      "advise": [
        {
          "selector": ".metadata .annotations .\"container.seccomp.security. \
                      alpha.kubernetes.io/pod\"",
          "reason": "Seccomp profiles set minimum privilege and secure against \
                     unknown threats"
        },
        {
          "selector": ".spec .serviceAccountName",
          "reason": "Service accounts restrict Kubernetes API access and should \
                     be configured with least privilege"
        },
        {
          "selector": ".metadata .annotations .\"container.apparmor.security. \
                      beta.kubernetes.io/nginx\"",
          "reason": "Well defined AppArmor policies may provide greater \
                     protection from unknown threats. WARNING: NOT PRODUCTION \
                     READY"
        }
      ]
    }
  }
]
```

Scanning Images for Known Vulnerabilities

One of the top sources for logging and discovering security vulnerabilities is CVE Details (*https://oreil.ly/DDlVa*). The page lists and ranks known vulnerabilities (CVEs) by score. Automated tooling can identify the software components embedded in a container image, compare those with the central vulnerabilities database, and flag issues by their severity.

One of the open source tools with this capability explicitly mentioned in the CKS curriculum is Trivy (*https://oreil.ly/hqPHH*). Trivy can run in different modes of operation: as a command line tool, in a container, as a GitHub Action configurable in a continuous integration workflow, as a plugin for the IDE VSCode, and as a Kubernetes operator. For an overview of the available installation options and procedures, see the Trivy documentation (*https://oreil.ly/qB_c8*). During the exam, you are not expected to install the tool. It will already be preconfigured for you. All you need to understand is how to run it and how to interpret and fix the found vulnerabilities.

Say you installed the command line implementation of Trivy. You can check the version of Trivy with the following command:

```
$ trivy -v
Version: 0.36.1
Vulnerability DB:
  Version: 2
  UpdatedAt: 2022-12-13 12:07:14.884952254 +0000 UTC
  NextUpdate: 2022-12-13 18:07:14.884951854 +0000 UTC
  DownloadedAt: 2022-12-13 17:09:28.866739 +0000 UTC
```

As you can see in Figure 6-7, Trivy indicates the timestamp when a copy of known vulnerabilities has been downloaded from the central database. Trivy can scan container images in various forms. The subcommand `image` simply expects you to spell out the image name and tag, in this case `python:3.4-alpine`.

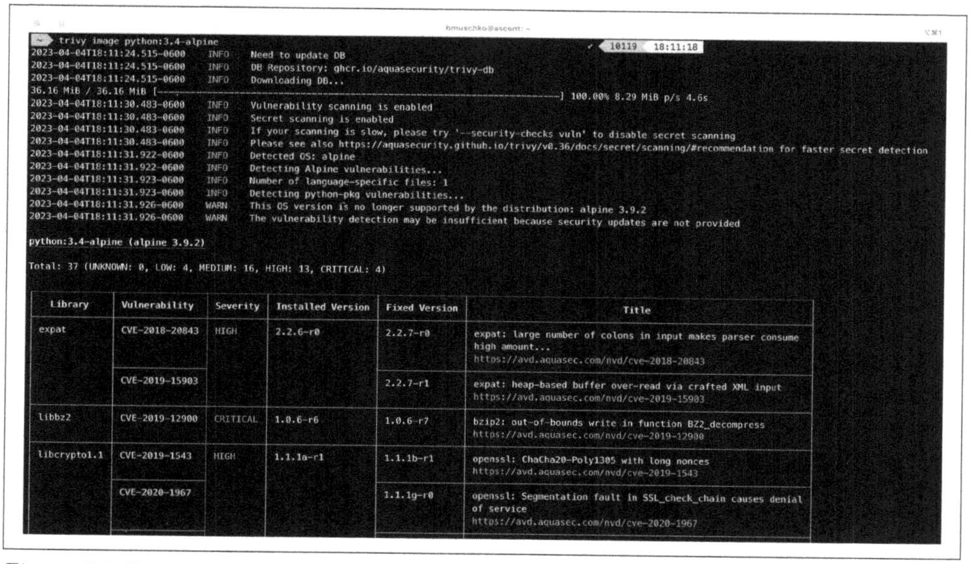

Figure 6-7. Reporting generated by scanning a container image with Trivy

The most important information in the output consists of the library that contains a specific vulnerability, its severity, and the minimum version to use that fixes the issue. Any found vulnerabilities with high or critical severity should be considered for a fix. If you do not have any control over the container image yourself, you can try to upgrade to a newer version.

Summary

Kubernetes primary objective is to run applications in containers in a scalable and secure fashion. In this chapter, we looked at the process, best practices, and tooling that help to ensure that a container image is produced that is small in size and that ships with as few known security vulnerabilities as possible.

We reviewed some of the most efficient techniques to reduce the footprint of a container image to a minimum. Start by picking a small base image to start with. You can even go to the extreme and not provide a shell at all for additional gains in size reduction. If you are using Docker, you can leverage the multi-stage approach that lets you build the application inside of the container without bundling the compiler, runtime, and build tools necessary to achieve the goal.

When consuming the container image in a Pod, make sure to only pull the container image from a trusted registry. It's advisable to set up an in-house container registry to serve up container images, so that reaching out to public, internet-accessible registries becomes obsolete, to eliminate potential security risks. You can enforce the usage of a list of trusted container registries with the help of OPA Gatekeeper. Another measure of security can be enforced by using the SHA256 hash of a container image to validate its expected contents.

The process of building and scanning a container image can be incorporated into a CI/CD pipeline. Third-party tools can parse and analyze the resource files of your deployable artifacts even before you build them. We looked at Haskell Dockerfile Linter for Dockerfiles and Kubesec for Kubernetes manifests. The other use case that needs to be covered on security aspects is consuming an existing container image built by an entity external to you as a developer, or your company. Before running a container image in a Kubernetes Pod, make sure to scan the contents for vulnerabilities. Trivy is one of those tools that can identify and report vulnerabilities in a container image to give you an idea of the security risks you are exposing yourself to in case you are planning to operate it in a container.

Exam Essentials

Become familiar with techniques that help with reducing the container image footprint.
In this section, we described some techniques for reducing the size of a container image when building it. I would suggest you read the best practices mentioned

on the Docker web page and try to apply them to sample container images. Compare the size of the produced container image before and after applying a technique. You can try to challenge yourself by reducing a container image to the smallest size possible while at the same time avoiding the loss of crucial functionality.

Walk through the process of governing where a container image can be resolved from.
OPA Gatekeeper offers a way to define the registries users are allowed to resolve container images from. Set up the objects for the constraint template and constraint, and see if the rules apply properly for a Pod that defines a main application container, an init container, and an ephemeral container. To broaden your exposure, also look at other products in the Kubernetes spaces that provide similar functionality. One of those products is Kyverno (*https://kyverno.io*).

Sign a container image and verify it using the hash.
After building a container image, make sure to also create a digest for it. Publish the container image, as well as the digest, to a registry. Practice how to use the digest in a Pod definition and verify the behavior of Kubernetes upon pulling the container image.

Understand how to configure the ImagePolicyWebhook admission controller plugin.
You are not expected to write a backend for an ImagePolicyWebhook. That's out of scope for the exam and requires knowledge of a programming language. You do need to understand how to enable the plugin in the API server configuration, though. I would suggest you practice the workflow even if you don't have a running backend application available.

Know how to fix warnings produced by static analysis tools.
The CKS curriculum doesn't prescribe a specific tool for analyzing Dockerfiles and Kubernetes manifests. During the exam, you may be asked to run a specific command that will produce a list of error and/or warning messages. Understand how to interpret the messages, and how to fix them in the relevant resource files.

Practice the use of Trivy to identify and fix security vulnerabilities.
The FAQ of the CKS lists the documentation page for Trivy. Therefore, it's fair to assume that Trivy may come up in one of the questions. You will need to understand the different ways to invoke Trivy to scan a container image. The produced report will give a you clear indication on what needs to be fixed and the severity of the found vulnerability. Given that you can't modify the container image easily, you will likely be asked to flag Pods that run container images with known vulnerabilities.

Sample Exercises

Solutions to these exercises are available in the Appendix.

1. Have a look at the following Dockerfile. Can you identify possibilities for reducing the footprint of the produced container image?

   ```
   FROM node:latest
   ENV NODE_ENV development
   WORKDIR /app
   COPY package.json .
   RUN npm install
   COPY . .
   EXPOSE 3001
   CMD ["node", "app.js"]
   ```

   Apply Dockerfile best practices to optimize the container image footprint. Run the docker build command before and after making optimizations. The resulting size of the container image should be smaller but the application should still be functioning.

2. Install Kyverno in your Kubernetes cluster. You can find installation instructions in the documentation (*https://oreil.ly/yxlLe*).

   Apply the "Restrict Image Registries" policy described on the documentation page (*https://oreil.ly/Kdj1k*). The only allowed registry should be gcr.io. Usage of any other registry should be denied.

   Create a Pod that defines the container image gcr.io/google-containers/busybox:1.27.2. Creation of the Pod should fail. Create another Pod using the container image busybox:1.27.2. Kyverno should allow the Pod to be created.

3. Define a Pod using the container image nginx:1.23.3-alpine in the YAML manifest pod-validate-image.yaml. Retrieve the digest of the container image from Docker Hub. Validate the container image contents using the SHA256 hash. Create the Pod. Kubernetes should be able to successfully pull the container image.

4. Use Kubesec to analyze the following contents of the YAML manifest file pod.yaml:

   ```
   apiVersion: v1
   kind: Pod
   metadata:
     name: hello-world
   spec:
     securityContext:
       runAsUser: 0
     containers:
   ```

```
- name: linux
  image: hello-world:linux
```

Inspect the suggestions generated by Kubesec. Ignore the suggestions on seccomp and AppArmor. Fix the root cause of all messages so that another execution of the tool will not report any additional suggestions.

5. Navigate to the directory *app-a/ch06/trivy* of the checked-out GitHub repository *bmuschko/cks-study-guide* (*https://oreil.ly/sImXZ*). Execute the command `kubectl apply -f setup.yaml`.

The command creates three different Pods in the namespace `r61`. From the command line, execute Trivy against the container images used by the Pods. Delete all Pods that have "CRITICAL" vulnerabilities. Which of the Pods are still running?

CHAPTER 7

Monitoring, Logging, and Runtime Security

The last domain of the curriculum primarily deals with detecting suspicious activity on the host and container level in a Kubernetes cluster. We'll first define the term *behavior analytics* and how it applies to the realm of Kubernetes. With the theory out of the way, we'll bring in the tool called Falco that can detect intrusion scenarios.

Once a container has been started, its runtime environment can still be modified. For example, as an operator you could decide to shell into the container in order to manually install additional tools or write files to the container's temporary filesystem. Modifying a container after it has been started can open doors to security risks. You will want to aim for creating *immutable containers*, containers that cannot be modified after they have been started. We'll learn how to configure a Pod with the right settings to make its containers immutable.

Last, we'll talk about capturing logs for events that occur in a Kubernetes cluster. Those logs can be used for troubleshooting purposes on the cluster level, to reconstruct when and how the cluster configuration was changed such that it led to an undesired or broken runtime behavior. Log entries can also be used to trace an attack that may be happening right now as a means to enacting countermeasures.

At a high level, this chapter covers the following concepts:

- Performing behavior analytics to detect malicious activities
- Performing deep analytical investigation and identification
- Ensuring immutability of containers at runtime
- Using audit logs to monitor access

Performing Behavior Analytics

Apart from managing and upgrading a Kubernetes cluster, the administrator is in charge of keeping an eye on potentially malicious activity. While you can perform this task manually by logging into cluster nodes and observing host- and container-level processes, it is a horribly inefficient undertaking.

Behavior analytics is the process of observing the cluster nodes for any activity that seems out of the ordinary. An automated process helps with filtering, recording, and alerting events of specific interest.

Scenario: A Kubernetes Administrator Can Observe Actions Taken by an Attacker

An attacker gained access to a container by opening a shell running on a worker node to launch additional attacks throughout the Kubernetes cluster. An administrator can't easily detect this event by manually checking each and every container. Figure 7-1 illustrates the scenario.

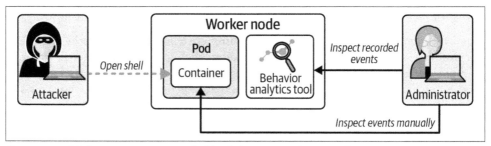

Figure 7-1. Malicious events recorded by behavior analytics tool

The administrator decided to take matters in their own hands by installing a behavior analytics tool. The tool will continuously monitor certain events and record them almost instantaneously. The administrator now has an efficient mechanism for detecting intrusions and can act upon them.

Among the behavior analytics tools relevant to the exam are Falco (*https://falco.org*), Tracee (*https://oreil.ly/ibXcO*), and Tetragon (*https://oreil.ly/q15oU*). In this book, we'll only focus on Falco, as it is listed among the links of documentation pages available during the exam.

Understanding Falco

Falco helps with detecting threats by observing host- and container-level activity. Here are a few examples of events Falco could watch for:

- Reading or writing files at specific locations in the filesystem
- Opening a shell binary for a container, such as `/bin/bash` to open a bash shell
- An attempt to make a network call to undesired URLs

Falco deploys a set of sensors that listen for the configured events and conditions. Each sensor consists of a set of rules that map an event to a data source. An alert is produced when a rule matches a specific event. Alerts will be sent to an output channel to record the event, such as standard output, a file, or an HTTPS endpoint. Falco allows for enabling more than one output channel simultaneously. Figure 7-2 shows Falco's high-level architecture.

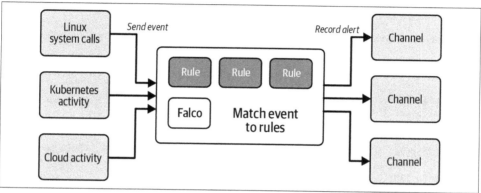

Figure 7-2. Falco's high-level architecture

Falco is a tool with a lot of features and configuration options. We won't be able to discuss all features in this book, but I would suggest you spend some time on understanding Falco's high-level concepts.

Another great learning resource on Falco can be found on the Sysdig training portal webpage. "Falco 101" (*https://oreil.ly/PwGWx*) is a free video course that explains all the bells and whistles of the product. All you need to do to get started is sign up for an account. Moreover, I'd suggest giving the book *Practical Cloud Native Security with Falco* by Loris Degioanni and Leonardo Grasso (O'Reilly) a read. The content takes a beginner-friendly approach to learning Falco.

Installing Falco

Falco can be installed as a binary on the host system or as a DaemonSet object in Kubernetes. You can safely assume that Falco has been preinstalled for you in the exam environment. For more information on the installation process, have a look at the relevant portion (*https://oreil.ly/MB6wU*) of the Falco documentation. The following steps briefly explain the installation of the binary on an Ubuntu machine.

Falco needs to be installed on all worker nodes of a Kubernetes cluster. Be aware that those instructions may change with a future version of Falco.

First, you need to trust the Falco GPG key, configure the Falco-specific apt repository, and update the package list:

```
$ curl -s https://falco.org/repo/falcosecurity-packages.asc | apt-key add -
$ echo "deb https://download.falco.org/packages/deb stable main" | tee -a \
  /etc/apt/sources.list.d/falcosecurity.list
$ apt-get update -y
```

You then install the kernel header with the following command:

```
$ apt-get -y install linux-headers-$(uname -r)
```

Last, you need to install the Falco apt package with version 0.33.1:

```
$ apt-get install -y falco=0.33.1
```

Falco has been installed successfully and is running as a systemd service in the background. Run the following command to check on the status of the Falco service:

```
$ sudo systemctl status falco
● falco.service - Falco: Container Native Runtime Security
     Loaded: loaded (/lib/systemd/system/falco.service; enabled; vendor preset: \
             enabled)
     Active: active (running) since Tue 2023-01-24 15:42:31 UTC; 43min ago
       Docs: https://falco.org/docs/
   Main PID: 8718 (falco)
      Tasks: 12 (limit: 1131)
     Memory: 30.2M
     CGroup: /system.slice/falco.service
             └─8718 /usr/bin/falco --pidfile=/var/run/falco.pid
```

The Falco service should be in the "active" status. It is already monitoring events in your system.

Configuring Falco

The Falco service provides an operational environment for monitoring the system with a set of default rules. Those rules live in YAML files in the /etc/falco directory. The list of files and subdirectories in /etc/falco is as follows:

```
$ tree /etc/falco
/etc/falco
├── aws_cloudtrail_rules.yaml
├── falco.yaml
├── falco_rules.local.yaml
├── falco_rules.yaml
├── k8s_audit_rules.yaml
├── rules.available
│   └── application_rules.yaml
└── rules.d
```

Of those files, I want to describe the high-level purpose of the most important ones.

Falco configuration file

The file named `falco.yaml` is the configuration file for the Falco process. It controls the channel that will be notified in case of an alert. A channel could be standard output or a file. Furthermore, the file defines the minimum log level of alerts to include in logs, and how to configure the embedded web server used to implement a health check for the Falco process. Refer to "Falco Configuration Options" (*https://oreil.ly/sfHW9*) for a full reference on all available options.

Default rules

The file named `falco_rules.yaml` defines a set of preinstalled rules. Falco considers those rules to be applied by default. Among them are checks for creating an alert when a shell to a container is opened or when a write operation is performed to a system directory. You can find other examples and their corresponding rule definitions on the "Rules Examples" page (*https://oreil.ly/fxHQm*).

Custom rules

The file named `falco_rules.local.yaml` lets you define custom rules and override default rules. With a fresh installation of Falco, the file only contains commented-out rules to provide you with a starting point for adding your own rules. You can find guidance on writing custom rules (*https://oreil.ly/mJnPo*) in the Falco documentation.

Kubernetes-specific rules

The file `k8s_audit_rules.yaml` defines Kubernetes-specific rules (*https://oreil.ly/d5FGD*) in addition to logging system call events. Typical examples are "log an event when a namespace is deleted" or "log an event when a Role or ClusterRole object is created."

Applying configuration changes

Modifying the contents of configuration files will not automatically propagate them to the Falco process. You need to restart the Falco service, as demonstrated by the following command:

```
$ sudo systemctl restart falco
```

Next up, we'll trigger some of the events covered by Falco's default rules. Each of those events will create an alert written to the configured channel. The initial setup of Falco routes messages to standard output.

Generating Events and Inspecting Falco Logs

Let's see Falco alerts in action. One of the default rules added by Falco creates an alert whenever a user tries to open a shell to a container. We'll need to perform this activity to see a log entry for it. To achieve that, create a new Pod named nginx, open a bash shell to the container, and then exit out of the container:

```
$ kubectl run nginx --image=nginx:1.23.3
pod/nginx created
$ kubectl exec -it nginx -- bash
root@nginx:/# exit
```

Identify the cluster node the Pod runs on by inspecting its runtime details:

```
$ kubectl get pod nginx -o jsonpath='{.spec.nodeName}'
kube-worker-1
```

This Pod is running on the cluster node named kube-worker-1. You will need to inspect the Falco logs on that machine to find the relevant log entry. You can inspect logged events by using the journalctl command directly on the kube-worker-1 cluster node. The following command searches for entries that contain the keyword falco:

```
$ sudo journalctl -fu falco
...
Jan 24 18:03:37 kube-worker-1 falco[8718]: 18:03:14.632368639: Notice A shell \
was spawned in a container with an attached terminal (user=root user_loginuid=0 \
nginx (id=18b247adb3ca) shell=bash parent=runc cmdline=bash pid=47773 \
terminal=34816 container_id=18b247adb3ca image=docker.io/library/nginx)
```

You will find that additional rules will kick in if you try to modify the container state. Say you'd installed the Git package using apt in the nginx container:

```
root@nginx:/# apt update
root@nginx:/# apt install git
```

Falco added log entries for those system-level operations. The following output renders the alerts:

```
$ sudo journalctl -fu falco
Jan 24 18:55:48 ubuntu-focal falco[8718]: 18:55:05.173895727: Error Package \
management process launched in container (user=root user_loginuid=0 \
command=apt update pid=60538 container_id=18b247adb3ca container_name=nginx \
image=docker.io/library/nginx:1.23.3)
Jan 24 18:55:48 ubuntu-focal falco[8718]: 18:55:11.050925982: Error Package \
management process launched in container (user=root user_loginuid=0 \
command=apt install git-all pid=60823 container_id=18b247adb3ca \
container_name=nginx image=docker.io/library/nginx:1.23.3)
...
```

In the next section, we'll inspect the Falco rules that trigger the creation of alerts, and their syntax.

Understanding Falco Rule File Basics

A Falco rules file usually consists of three elements defined in YAML: rules, macros, and lists. You'll need to understand those elements on a high level and know how to modify them to achieve a certain goal.

Crafting your own Falco rules

During the exam, you will likely not have to craft your own Falco rules. You'll be provided with an existing set of rules. If you want to dive deeper into Falco rules, have a look at the relevant documentation page (*https://oreil.ly/PD1ro*).

Rule

A *rule* is the condition under which an alert should be generated. It also defines the output message of the alert. An output message can consist of a hard-coded message and incorporate built-in variables. The alert is recorded on the WARNING log level. Example 7-1 shows the YAML for a rule listening to events that try to access the machine's camera from processes other than your traditional video-conferencing software, such as Skype or Webex.

Example 7-1. A Falco rule that monitors camera access

```
- rule: access_camera
  desc: a process other than skype/webex tries to access the camera
  condition: evt.type = open and fd.name = /dev/video0 and not proc.name in \
          (skype, webex)
  output: Unexpected process opening camera video device (command=%proc.cmdline)
  priority: WARNING
```

Macro

A *macro* is a reusable rule condition that helps with avoiding copy-pasting similar logic across multiple rules. Macros are useful if the rule file becomes lengthy and you want to improve on maintainability.

Say you are in the process of simplifying a rules file. You notice that multiple rules use the same condition that listens for camera access. Example 7-2 shows how to break out the logic into a macro.

Example 7-2. A Falco macro defining a reusable condition

```
- macro: camera_process_access
  condition: evt.type = open and fd.name = /dev/video0 and not proc.name in \
          (skype, webex)
```

The macro can now be referenced by name in a rule definition, as shown in Example 7-3.

Example 7-3. A Falco rule incorporating a macro

```
- rule: access_camera
  desc: a process other than skype/webex tries to access the camera
  condition: camera_process_access
  output: Unexpected process opening camera video device (command=%proc.cmdline)
  priority: WARNING
```

List

A *list* is a collection of items that you can include in rules, macros, and other lists. Think of lists as an array in traditional programming languages. Example 7-4 creates a list of process names associated with video-conferencing software.

Example 7-4. A Falco list

```
- list: video_conferencing_software
  items: [skype, webex]
```

Example 7-5 shows the usage of the list by name in a macro.

Example 7-5. A Falco macro that uses a list

```
- macro: camera_process_access
  condition: evt.type = open and fd.name = /dev/video0 and not proc.name in \
          (video_conferencing_software)
```

Dissecting an existing rule

The reason why Falco ships with default rules is to shorten the timespan to hit the ground running for a production cluster. Instead of having to come up with your own rules and the correct syntax, you can simply install Falco and benefit from best practices from the get-go.

Let's come back to one of the events we triggered in "Generating Events and Inspecting Falco Logs" on page 146. At the time of writing, I am using the Falco version 0.33.1. The rules file /etc/falco/falco_rules.yaml shipped with it contains a rule named "Terminal shell in container." It observes the event of opening a shell to a container. You can easily find the rule by searching for a portion of the log message, e.g., "A shell was spawned in a container." Example 7-6 shows the syntax of the rule definition, as well as the annotated portions of the YAML.

Example 7-6. A Falco rule that monitors shell activity to a container

```
- macro: spawned_process ❶
  condition: (evt.type in (execve, execveat) and evt.dir=<)

- macro: container ❶
  condition: (container.id != host)

- macro: container_entrypoint ❶
  condition: (not proc.pname exists or proc.pname in (runc:[0:PARENT], \
              runc:[1:CHILD], runc, docker-runc, exe, docker-runc-cur))

- macro: user_expected_terminal_shell_in_container_conditions ❶
  condition: (never_true)

- rule: Terminal shell in container ❷
  desc: A shell was used as the entrypoint/exec point into a container with an \
        attached terminal.
  condition: > ❸
    spawned_process and container
    and shell_procs and proc.tty != 0
    and container_entrypoint
    and not user_expected_terminal_shell_in_container_conditions
  output: > ❹
    A shell was spawned in a container with an attached terminal (user=%user.name \
    user_loginuid=%user.loginuid %container.info
    shell=%proc.name parent=%proc.pname cmdline=%proc.cmdline pid=%proc.pid \
    terminal=%proc.tty container_id=%container.id image=%container.image.repository)
  priority: NOTICE ❺
  tags: [container, shell, mitre_execution] ❻
```

❶ Defines a macro, a condition reusable across multiple rules referenced by name.

❷ Specifies the name of the rule.

❸ The aggregated condition composed of multiple macros.

❹ The alerting message should the event happen. The message may use built-in fields to reference runtime value.

❺ Indicates how serious a violation of the rule it is.

❻ Categorizes the rule set into groups of related rules for ease of management.

Sometimes you may want to change an existing rule. The next section will explain how to best approach overriding default rules.

Overriding Existing Rules

Instead of modifying the rule definition directly in /etc/falco/falco_rules.yaml, I'd suggest you redefine the rule in /etc/falco/falco_rules.local.yaml. That'll help with falling back to the original rule definition in case you want to get rid of the modifications or if you make any mistakes in the process. The rule definition needs to be changed on all worker nodes of the cluster.

The rule definition shown in Example 7-7 overrides the rule named "Terminal shell in container" by changing the priority to ALERT and the output to a new format by incorporating built-in fields (*https://oreil.ly/z5oAk*).

Example 7-7. The modified rule that monitors shell activity to a container

```
- rule: Terminal shell in container
  desc: A shell was used as the entrypoint/exec point into a container with an \
        attached terminal.
  condition: >
    spawned_process and container
    and shell_procs and proc.tty != 0
    and container_entrypoint
    and not user_expected_terminal_shell_in_container_conditions
  output: >
    Opened shell: %evt.time,%user.name,%container.name ❶
  priority: ALERT ❷
  tags: [container, shell, mitre_execution]
```

❶ Simplifies the log output rendered for a violation.

❷ Treats a violation of the rule with ALERT priority.

After adding the rule to falco_rules.local.yaml, we need to let Falco pick up the changes. Restart the Falco service with the following command:

```
$ sudo systemctl restart falco
```

As a result, any attempt that shells into a container will be logged with a different output format and priority, as the following shows:

```
$ sudo journalctl -fu falco
...
Jan 24 21:19:13 kube-worker-1 falco[100017]: 21:19:13.961970887: Alert Opened \
shell: 21:19:13.961970887,<NA>,nginx
```

In addition to overriding existing Falco rules, you can also define your own custom rules in /etc/falco/falco_rules.local.yaml. Writing custom rules is out of scope for this book, but you should find plenty of information on the topic in the Falco documentation.

Ensuring Container Immutability

Containers are mutable by default. After the container has been started, you can open a shell to it, install a patch for existing software, modify files, or make changes to its configuration. Mutable containers allow attackers to gain access to the container by downloading or installing malicious software.

To counteract the situation, make sure that the container is operated in an immutable state. That means preventing write operations to the container's filesystem or even disallowing shell access to the container. If you need to make any substantial changes to the container, such as updating a dependency or incorporating a new application feature, you should release a new tag of the container image instead of manually modifying the container itself. You'd then assign the new tag of the container image to the Pod without having to modify the internals directly.

Scenario: An Attacker Installs Malicious Software

Figure 7-3 illustrates a scenario where an attacker gains access to a container using stolen credentials. The attacker downloads and installs malicious software given that the container allows write operations to the root filesystem. The malicious software keeps monitoring activities in the container; for example, it could parse the application logs for sensitive information. It may then send the information to a server outside of the Kubernetes cluster. Consequently, the data is used as a means to log into other parts of the system.

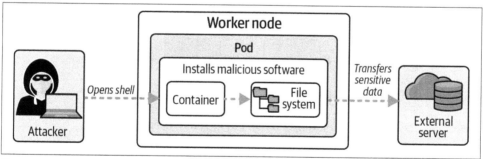

Figure 7-3. An attacker shells into a container and installs malicious software

In the next section, you'll learn how to prevent the situation from happening by using a distroless container image, injecting configuration data with the help of a ConfigMap or Secret, and by configuring a read-only container filesystem. Those settings as a whole will make the container truly immutable.

Using a Distroless Container Image

Distroless container images have become increasing popular in the world of containers. They only bundle your application and its runtime dependencies, while at the same time removing as much of the operating system as possible, e.g., shells, package managers, and libraries. Distroless container images are not just smaller in size; they are also more secure. An attacker cannot shell into the container, and therefore the filesystem cannot be misused to install malicious software. Using distroless container images is the first line of defense in creating an immutable container. We already covered distroless container images in "Picking a Base Image Small in Size" on page 114. Refer to that section for more information.

Configuring a Container with a ConfigMap or Secret

It is best practice to use the same container image for different deployment environments, even though their runtime configurations may be different. Any environment-specific configuration, such as credentials, and connection URLs to other parts of the system, should be externalized. In Kubernetes, you can inject configuration data into a container with the help of a ConfigMap or Secret as environment variables or files mounted via Volumes. Figure 7-4 shows the reuse of the same container image to configure a Pod in a development and production cluster. Configuration data specific to the environment is provided by a ConfigMap.

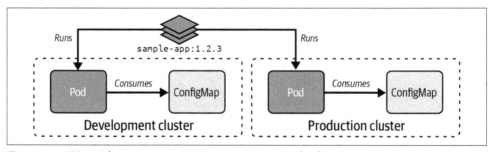

Figure 7-4. Using the same container image across multiple environments

Avoiding the creation of environment-specific container images simplifies the creation process, reduces the risk of introducing accidental security risks, and makes testing of the functionality easier. Injecting runtime values does not require changing the container after it has been started and therefore is key to making it immutable.

When using Secrets as environment variables in a container, make sure to avoid accidentally logging the values to standard output, e.g., as a plain-text value when writing a log message. Anyone with access to the container logs would be able to parse them for Secrets values. As a spot check, identify the places in your application code where you use a Secret and assess their risk for exposure.

To brush up on creating, configuring, and consuming ConfigMaps and Secrets, revisit the Kubernetes documentation (*https://oreil.ly/RjxjE*).

Configuring a Read-Only Container Root Filesystem

Another aspect of container immutability is to prevent write access to the container's filesystem. You can configure this runtime behavior by assigning the value `true` to the attribute `spec.containers[].securityContext.readOnlyRootFilesystem`.

There are some applications that still require write access to fulfill their functional requirements. For example, nginx (*https://www.nginx.com*) needs to write to the directories `/var/run`, `/var/cache/nginx`, and `/usr/local/nginx`. In combination with setting `readOnlyRootFilesystem` to `true`, you can declare Volumes that make those directories writable. Example 7-8 shows the YAML manifest of an immutable container running nginx.

Example 7-8. A container disallowing write access to the root filesystem

```
apiVersion: v1
kind: Pod
metadata:
  name: nginx
spec:
  containers:
  - name: nginx
    image: nginx:1.21.6
    securityContext:
      readOnlyRootFilesystem: true
    volumeMounts:
    - name: nginx-run
      mountPath: /var/run
    - name: nginx-cache
      mountPath: /var/cache/nginx
    - name: nginx-data
      mountPath: /usr/local/nginx
  volumes:
  - name: nginx-run
    emptyDir: {}
  - name: nginx-data
    emptyDir: {}
  - name: nginx-cache
    emptyDir: {}
```

Identify the filesystem read/write requirements of your application before creating a Pod. Configure write mountpaths with the help of Volumes. Any other filesystem path should become read-only.

Using Audit Logs to Monitor Access

It's imperative for a Kubernetes administrator to have a record of events that have occurred in the cluster. Those records can help detect an intrusion in real-time, or they can be used to track down configuration changes for troubleshooting purposes. *Audit logs* provide a chronological view of events received by the API server.

Scenario: An Administrator Can Monitor Malicious Events in Real Time

Figure 7-5 shows the benefits of monitoring Kubernetes API events. In this scenario, the attacker tries to make calls to the API server. Events of interest have been captured by the audit log mechanism. The administrator can view those events at any time, identify intrusion attempts, and take countermeasure.

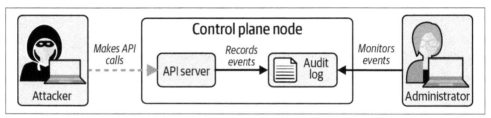

Figure 7-5. An attacker monitored by observing audit logs

We only reviewed one of the use cases here, the one that applies to security concerns. The ability to trace company-internal API requests should not be underestimated. By reviewing audit logs, the administrator can provide guidance to application developers trying to create Kubernetes objects, or reconstruct configuration changes that may have led to faulty cluster behavior.

Understanding Audit Logs

Kubernetes can store records for events triggered by end users for any requests made to the API server or for events emitted by the control plane itself. Entries in the audit log exist in JSON Lines (*https://jsonlines.org*) format and can consist of, but aren't limited to, the following information:

- What event occurred?
- Who triggered the event?
- When was it triggered?
- Which Kubernetes component handled the request?

The type of event and the corresponding request data to be recorded are defined by an *audit policy*. The audit policy is a YAML manifest specifying those rules and has to be provided to the API server process.

The *audit backend* is responsible for storing the recorded audit events, as defined by the audit policy. You have two configurable options for a backend:

- A log backend, which write the events to a file.
- A webhook backend, which sends the events to an external service via HTTP(S)—for example, for the purpose of integrating a centralized logging and monitoring system. Such a backend can help with debugging runtime issues like a crashed application.

Figure 7-6 puts together all the pieces necessary to configure audit logging. The following sections will explain the details of configuring them.

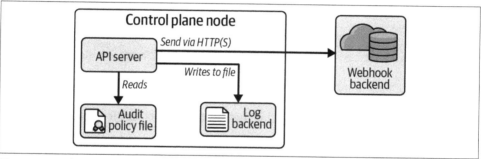

Figure 7-6. The high-level audit log architecture

Let's have a deeper look at the audit policy file and its configuration options.

Creating the Audit Policy File

The audit policy file is effectively a YAML manifest for a `Policy` resource. Any event received by the API server is matched against the rules defined in the policy file in the order of definition. The event is logged with the declared audit level if a matching rule can be found. Table 7-1 lists all available audit levels.

Table 7-1. Audit levels

Level	Effect
None	Do not log events matching this rule.
Metadata	Only log request metadata for the event.
Request	Log metadata and the request body for the event.
RequestResponse	Log metadata, request, and response body for the event.

Example 7-9 shows an exemplary audit policy. The rules are specified as an array of items with the attribute named rules. Each rule declares a level, the resource type and API group it applies to, and an optional namespace.

Example 7-9. Contents of an audit policy file

```
apiVersion: audit.k8s.io/v1
kind: Policy
omitStages:
  - "RequestReceived" ❶
rules:
  - level: RequestResponse ❷
    resources:
    - group: ""
      resources: ["pods"]
  - level: Metadata ❸
    resources:
    - group: ""
      resources: ["pods/log", "pods/status"]
```

❶ Prevents generating logs for all requests in the RequestReceived stage

❷ Logs Pod changes at RequestResponse level

❸ Logs specialized Pod events, e.g., log and status requests, at the Metadata level

The previous audit policy isn't very extensive but should give you an impression of its format. Refer to the Kubernetes documentation (*https://oreil.ly/Zozkf*) for additional examples and more details.

Once the audit policy file has been created, it can be consumed by the API server process. Add the flag --audit-policy-file to the API server process in the file /etc/kubernetes/manifests/kube-apiserver.yaml. The value assigned to the parameter is the fully qualified path to the audit policy file.

Next up, we'll walk through the settings needed to configure audit logging for the API server for a file-based log backend and a webhook backend.

Configuring a Log Backend

To set up a file-based log backend, you will need to add three pieces of configuration to the file /etc/kubernetes/manifests/kube-apiserver.yaml. The following list summarizes the configuration:

1. Provide two flags to the API server process: the flag --audit-policy-file points to the audit policy file; the flag --audit-log-path points to the log output file.

2. Add a Volume mountpath for the audit log policy file and the log output directory.

3. Add a Volume definition to the host path for the audit log policy file and the log output directory.

Example 7-10 shows the modified content of the API server configuration file.

Example 7-10. Configuring the audit policy file and audit log file

```
...
spec:
  containers:
  - command:
    - kube-apiserver
    - --audit-policy-file=/etc/kubernetes/audit-policy.yaml ❶
    - --audit-log-path=/var/log/kubernetes/audit/audit.log ❶
    ...
    volumeMounts:
    - mountPath: /etc/kubernetes/audit-policy.yaml ❷
      name: audit
      readOnly: true
    - mountPath: /var/log/kubernetes/audit/ ❷
      name: audit-log
      readOnly: false
  ...
  volumes:
  - name: audit ❸
    hostPath:
      path: /etc/kubernetes/audit-policy.yaml
      type: File
  - name: audit-log ❸
    hostPath:
      path: /var/log/kubernetes/audit/
      type: DirectoryOrCreate
```

❶ Provides the location of the policy file and log file to the API server process.

❷ Mounts the policy file and the audit log directory to the given paths.

❸ Defines the Volumes for the policy file and the audit log directory.

The runtime behavior of the log backend can be further customized by passing additional flags to the API server process. For example, you can specify the maximum number of days to retain old audit log files by providing the flag `--audit-log-maxage`. Refer to the Kubernetes documentation (*https://oreil.ly/L-63d*) to have a look at the complete list of flags.

It's time to produce some log entries. The following `kubectl` command sends a request to the API server for creating a Pod named `nginx`:

```
$ kubectl run nginx --image=nginx:1.21.6
pod/nginx created
```

In the previous step, we configured the audit log file at `/var/log/kubernetes/audit/audit.log`. Depending on the rules in the audit policy, the number of entries may be overwhelming, which makes finding a specific event hard. A simple way to filter configured events is by searching for the value `audit.k8s.io/v1` assigned to the `apiVersion` attribute. The following command finds relevant log entries, one for the `RequestResponse` level, and another for the `Metadata` level:

```
$ sudo grep 'audit.k8s.io/v1' /var/log/kubernetes/audit/audit.log
...
{"kind":"Event","apiVersion":"audit.k8s.io/v1","level":"RequestResponse", \
"auditID":"285f4b99-951e-405b-b5de-6b66295074f4","stage":"ResponseComplete", \
"requestURI":"/api/v1/namespaces/default/pods/nginx","verb":"get", \
"user":{"username":"system:node:node01","groups":["system:nodes", \
"system:authenticated"]},"sourceIPs":["172.28.116.6"],"userAgent": \
"kubelet/v1.26.0 (linux/amd64) kubernetes/b46a3f8","objectRef": \
{"resource":"pods","namespace":"default","name":"nginx","apiVersion":"v1"}, \
"responseStatus":{"metadata":{},"code":200},"responseObject":{"kind":"Pod", \
"apiVersion":"v1","metadata":{"name":"nginx","namespace":"default", \
...
{"kind":"Event","apiVersion":"audit.k8s.io/v1","level":"Metadata","auditID": \
"5c8e5ecc-0ce0-49e0-8ab2-368284f2f785","stage":"ResponseComplete", \
"requestURI":"/api/v1/namespaces/default/pods/nginx/status","verb":"patch", \
"user":{"username":"system:node:node01","groups":["system:nodes", \
"system:authenticated"]},"sourceIPs":["172.28.116.6"],"userAgent": \
"kubelet/v1.26.0 (linux/amd64) kubernetes/b46a3f8","objectRef": \
{"resource":"pods","namespace":"default","name":"nginx","apiVersion":"v1", \
"subresource":"status"},"responseStatus":{"metadata":{},"code":200}, \
...
```

Configuring a Webhook Backend

Configuring a webhook backend looks different from configuring a log backend. We need to tell the API server to send an HTTP(S) request to an external service instead of the file. The configuration to the external service, the webhook, and the credentials needed to authenticate are defined in a kubeconfig file (*https://oreil.ly/bUnmO*), similarly to what we've done in "Configuring the ImagePolicyWebhook Admission Controller Plugin" on page 127.

Add the flag `--audit-webhook-config-file` to the API server process in the file `/etc/kubernetes/manifests/kube-apiserver.yaml`, and point it to the location of the kubeconfig file. The flag `--audit-webhook-initial-backoff` defines the time to wait after the initial request to the external service before retrying. You will still have to assign the flag `--audit-policy-file` to point to the audit policy file.

Summary

Monitoring and logging events in a Kubernetes cluster is an important duty of every administrator. We used Falco to identify and filter security-related events. You learned about the purpose and syntax of the different configuration files and how to find relevant alerts in the logs.

In addition to employing behavior analytics tools, you will want to set up audit logging for requests reaching the API server. Audit logging records configured events to a backend, either to a file on the control plane node or to an external service via an HTTP(S) call. We worked through the process of enabling audit logging for the API server process.

A sensible step toward more secure containers is to make them immutable. An immutable container only supports a read-only filesystem, so that a potential attacker cannot install malicious software. Mount a Volume if the application running inside of the container needs to write data. Use a distroless container image to lock out attackers from being able to shell into the container.

Exam Essentials

Practice how to configure and operate Falco.
Falco is definitely going to come up as a topic during the exam. You will need to understand how to read and modify a rule in a configuration file. I would suggest you browse through the syntax and options in more detail in case you need to write one yourself. The main entry point for running Falco is the command line tool. It's fair to assume that it will have been preinstalled in the exam environment.

Know how to identify immutable containers.
Immutable containers are a central topic to this exam domain. Understand how to set the `spec.containers[].securityContext.readOnlyRootFilesystem` attribute for a Pod and how to mount a Volume to a specific path in case a write operation is required by the container process.

Deeply understand audit log configuration options.
Setting up audit logging consists of two steps. For one, you need to understand the syntax and structure of an audit policy file. The other aspect is how to configure the API server to consume the audit policy file, provide a reference to a backend, and mount the relevant filesystem Volumes. Make sure to practice all of those aspects hands-on.

Sample Exercises

1. Navigate to the directory *app-a/ch07/falco* of the checked-out GitHub repository *bmuschko/cks-study-guide* (*https://oreil.ly/sImXZ*). Start up the VMs running the cluster using the command `vagrant up`. The cluster consists of a single control plane node named `kube-control-plane` and one worker node named `kube-worker-1`. Once done, shut down the cluster using `vagrant destroy -f`. Falco is already running as a systemd service.

   Inspect the process running in the existing Pod named `malicious`. Have a look at the Falco logs and see if a rule created a log for the process.

   Reconfigure the existing rule that creates a log for the event by changing the output to `<timestamp>,<username>,<container-id>`. Find the changed log entry in the Falco logs.

   Reconfigure Falco to write logs to the file at `/var/logs/falco.log`. Disable the standard output channel. Ensure that Falco appends new messages to the log file.

   Prerequisite: This exercise requires the installation of the tools Vagrant (*https://oreil.ly/FiyeH*) and VirtualBox (*https://oreil.ly/WW8IK*).

2. Navigate to the directory *app-a/ch07/immutable-container* of the checked-out GitHub repository *bmuschko/cks-study-guide* (*https://oreil.ly/sImXZ*). Execute the command `kubectl apply -f setup.yaml`.

   Inspect the Pod created by the YAML manifest in the `default` namespace. Make relevant changes to the Pod so that its container can be considered immutable.

3. Navigate to the directory *app-a/ch07/audit-log* of the checked-out GitHub repository *bmuschko/cks-study-guide* (*https://oreil.ly/sImXZ*). Start up the VMs running the cluster using the command `vagrant up`. The cluster consists of a single control plane node named `kube-control-plane` and one worker node named `kube-worker-1`. Once done, shut down the cluster using `vagrant destroy -f`.

   Edit the existing audit policy file at `/etc/kubernetes/audit/rules/audit-policy.yaml`. Add a rule that logs events for ConfigMaps and Secrets at the `Metadata` level. Add another rule that logs events for Services at the `Request` level.

   Configure the API server to consume the audit policy file. Logs should be written to the file `/var/log/kubernetes/audit/logs/apiserver.log`. Define a maximum number of five days to retain audit log files.

   Ensure that the log file has been created and contains at least one entry that matches the events configured.

   Prerequisite: This exercise requires the installation of the tools Vagrant (*https://oreil.ly/FiyeH*) and VirtualBox (*https://oreil.ly/WW8IK*).

Answers to Review Questions

Chapter 2, "Cluster Setup"

1. Create a file with the name `deny-egress-external.yaml` for defining the network policy. The network policy needs to set the Pod selector to `app=backend`
and define the `Egress` policy type. Make sure to allow the port 53 for the
protocols UDP and TCP. The namespace selector for the egress policy needs to
use {} to select all namespaces:

```
apiVersion: networking.k8s.io/v1
kind: NetworkPolicy
metadata:
  name: deny-egress-external
spec:
  podSelector:
    matchLabels:
      app: backend
  policyTypes:
  - Egress
  egress:
  - to:
    - namespaceSelector: {}
    ports:
    - port: 53
      protocol: UDP
    - port: 53
      protocol: TCP
```

Run the `apply` command to instantiate the network policy object from the YAML
file:

```
$ kubectl apply -f deny-egress-external.yaml
```

2. A Pod that does not match the label selection of the network policy can make a call to a URL outside of the cluster. In this case, the label assignment is app=frontend:

```
$ kubectl run web --image=busybox:1.36.0 -l app=frontend --port=80 -it \
  --rm --restart=Never -- wget http://google.com --timeout=5 --tries=1
Connecting to google.com (142.250.69.238:80)
Connecting to www.google.com (142.250.72.4:80)
saving to /'index.html'
index.html            100% |**| 13987 \
0:00:00 ETA
/'index.html' saved
pod "web" deleted
```

3. A Pod that does match the label selection of the network policy cannot make a call to a URL outside of the cluster. In this case, the label assignment is app=backend:

```
$ kubectl run web --image=busybox:1.36.0 -l app=backend --port=80 -it \
  --rm --restart=Never -- wget http://google.com --timeout=5 --tries=1
wget: download timed out
pod "web" deleted
pod default/web terminated (Error)
```

4. First, see if the Dashboard is already installed. You can check the namespace the Dashboard usually creates:

```
$ kubectl get ns kubernetes-dashboard
NAME                   STATUS   AGE
kubernetes-dashboard   Active   109s
```

If the namespace does not exist, you can assume that the Dashboard has not been installed yet. Install it with the following command:

```
$ kubectl apply -f https://raw.githubusercontent.com/kubernetes/\
dashboard/v2.6.0/aio/deploy/recommended.yaml
```

Create the ServiceAccount, ClusterRole, and ClusterRoleBinding. Make sure that the ClusterRole only allows listing Deployment objects. The following YAML manifest has been saved in the file dashboard-observer-user.yaml:

```
apiVersion: v1
kind: ServiceAccount
metadata:
  name: observer-user
  namespace: kubernetes-dashboard
---
apiVersion: rbac.authorization.k8s.io/v1
kind: ClusterRole
metadata:
  annotations:
    rbac.authorization.kubernetes.io/autoupdate: "true"
```

```
    name: cluster-observer
rules:
- apiGroups:
  - 'apps'
  resources:
  - 'deployments'
  verbs:
  - list
---
apiVersion: rbac.authorization.k8s.io/v1
kind: ClusterRoleBinding
metadata:
  name: observer-user
roleRef:
  apiGroup: rbac.authorization.k8s.io
  kind: ClusterRole
  name: cluster-observer
subjects:
- kind: ServiceAccount
  name: observer-user
  namespace: kubernetes-dashboard
```

Create the objects with the following command:

```
$ kubectl apply -f dashboard-observer-user.yaml
```

5. Run the following command to create a token for the ServiceAccount. The option `--duration 0s` ensures that the token will never expire. Copy the token that was rendered in the console output of the command:

```
$ kubectl create token observer-user -n kubernetes-dashboard \
  --duration 0s
eyJhbGciOiJSUzI1NiIsImtpZCI6Ik5lNFMxZ1...
```

Run the proxy command and open the link *http://localhost:8001/api/v1/namespaces/kubernetes-dashboard/services/https:kubernetes-dashboard:/proxy* in a browser:

```
$ kubectl proxy
```

Select the "Token" authentication method and paste the token you copied before. Sign into the Dashboard. You should see that only Deployment objects are listable (see Figure A-1).

All other objects will say "There is nothing to display here." Figure A-2 renders the list of Pods.

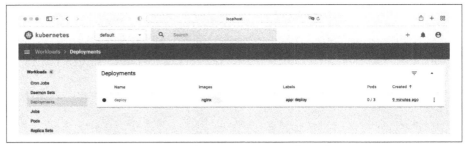

Figure A-1. The Dashboard view of Deployments is allowed

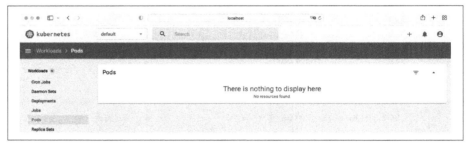

Figure A-2. The Dashboard view of Pods is not permitted

6. Download the API server binary with the following command:

```
$ curl -LO "https://dl.k8s.io/v1.26.1/bin/linux/amd64/kube-apiserver"
```

Next, download the SHA256 file for the same binary, but a different version. The following command downloads the file for version 1.23.1:

```
$ curl -LO "https://dl.k8s.io/v1.23.1/bin/linux/amd64/\
kube-apiserver.sha256"
```

Comparing the binary file with the checksum file results in a failure, as the versions do not match:

```
$ echo "$(cat kube-apiserver.sha256)  kube-apiserver" | shasum -a 256 \
  --check
kube-apiserver: FAILED
shasum: WARNING: 1 computed checksum did NOT match
```

Chapter 3, "Cluster Hardening"

1. Create a private key using the `openssl` executable. Provide an expressive file name, such as `jill.key`. The `-subj` option provides the username (CN) and the group (O). The following command uses the username `jill` and the group named `observer`:

```
$ openssl genrsa -out jill.key 2048
$ openssl req -new -key jill.key -out jill.csr -subj \
  "/CN=jill/O=observer"
```

Retrieve the base64-encoded value of the CSR file content with the following command. You will need it when creating a the CertificateSigningRequest object in the next step:

```
$ cat jill.csr | base64 | tr -d "\n"
LS0tLS1CRUdJTiBDRRVJUSUZJQ0FURSBSRVFVRVNULS0tL...
```

The following script creates a CertificateSigningRequest object:

```
$ cat <<EOF | kubectl apply -f -
apiVersion: certificates.k8s.io/v1
kind: CertificateSigningRequest
metadata:
  name: jill
spec:
  request: LS0tLS1CRUdJTiBDRRVJUSUZJQ0FURSBSRVFVRVNULS0tL...
  signerName: kubernetes.io/kube-apiserver-client
  expirationSeconds: 86400
  usages:
  - client auth
EOF
```

Use the `certificate approve` command to approve the signing request and export the issued certificate:

```
$ kubectl certificate approve jill
$ kubectl get csr jill -o jsonpath={.status.certificate}| base64 \
  -d > jill.crt
```

Add the user to the kubeconfig file and add the context for the user. The cluster name used here is minikube. It might be different for your Kubernetes environment:

```
$ kubectl config set-credentials jill --client-key=jill.key \
  --client-certificate=jill.crt --embed-certs=true
$ kubectl config set-context jill --cluster=minikube --user=jill
```

2. Create the Role and RoleBinding. The following imperative commands assign the verbs get, list, and watch for Pods, ConfigMaps, and Secrets to the subject named observer of type group. The user jill is part of the group:

```
$ kubectl create role observer --verb=create --verb=get --verb=list \
  --verb=watch --resource=pods --resource=configmaps --resource=secrets
$ kubectl create rolebinding observer-binding --role=observer \
  --group=observer
```

3. Switch to the user context:

```
$ kubectl config use-context jill
```

We'll pick one permitted operation, listing ConfigMap objects. The user is authorized to map the call:

```
$ kubectl get configmaps
NAME               DATA    AGE
kube-root-ca.crt   1       16m
```

Listing nodes won't be authorized. The user does not have the appropriate permissions:

```
$ kubectl get nodes
Error from server (Forbidden): nodes is forbidden: User "jill" cannot \
list resource "nodes" in API group "" at the cluster scope
```

Switch back to the admin context:

```
$ kubectl config use-context minikube
```

4. Create the namespace t23:

```
$ kubectl create namespace t23
```

Create the service account api-call in the namespace:

```
$ kubectl create serviceaccount api-call -n t23
```

Define a YAML manifest file with the name pod.yaml. The contents of the file define a Pod that makes an HTTPS GET call to the API server to retrieve the list of Services in the default namespace:

```
apiVersion: v1
kind: Pod
metadata:
  name: service-list
  namespace: t23
spec:
  serviceAccountName: api-call
  containers:
  - name: service-list
    image: alpine/curl:3.14
    command: ['sh', '-c', 'while true; do curl -s -k -m 5 \
             -H "Authorization: Bearer $(cat /var/run/secrets/\
             kubernetes.io/serviceaccount/token)" https://kubernetes.\
             default.svc.cluster.local/api/v1/namespaces/default/\
             services; sleep 10; done']
```

Create the Pod with the following command:

```
$ kubectl apply -f pod.yaml
```

Check the logs of the Pod. The API call is not authorized, as shown in the following log output:

```
$ kubectl logs service-list -n t23
{
```

```
  "kind": "Status",
  "apiVersion": "v1",
  "metadata": {},
  "status": "Failure",
  "message": "services is forbidden: User \"system:serviceaccount:t23 \
             :api-call\" cannot list resource \"services\" in API \
             group \"\" in the namespace \"default\"",
  "reason": "Forbidden",
  "details": {
    "kind": "services"
  },
  "code": 403
}
```

5. Create the YAML manifest in the file `clusterrole.yaml`, as shown in the following:

```
apiVersion: rbac.authorization.k8s.io/v1
kind: ClusterRole
metadata:
  name: list-services-clusterrole
rules:
- apiGroups: [""]
  resources: ["services"]
  verbs: ["list"]
```

Reference the ClusterRole in a RoleBinding defined in the file `rolebind ing.yaml`. The subject should list the service account `api-call` in the namespace t23:

```
apiVersion: rbac.authorization.k8s.io/v1
kind: RoleBinding
metadata:
  name: serviceaccount-service-rolebinding
subjects:
- kind: ServiceAccount
  name: api-call
  namespace: t23
roleRef:
  kind: ClusterRole
  name: list-services-clusterrole
  apiGroup: rbac.authorization.k8s.io
```

Create both objects from the YAML manifests:

```
$ kubectl apply -f clusterrole.yaml
$ kubectl apply -f rolebinding.yaml
```

The API call running inside of the container should now be authorized and be allowed to list the Service objects in the `default` namespace. As shown in the following output, the namespace currently hosts at least one Service object, the kubernetes.default Service:

```
$ kubectl logs service-list -n t23
{
  "kind": "ServiceList",
  "apiVersion": "v1",
  "metadata": {
    "resourceVersion": "1108"
  },
  "items": [
    {
      "metadata": {
        "name": "kubernetes",
        "namespace": "default",
        "uid": "30eb5425-8f60-4bb7-8331-f91fe0999e20",
        "resourceVersion": "199",
        "creationTimestamp": "2022-09-08T18:06:52Z",
        "labels": {
          "component": "apiserver",
          "provider": "kubernetes"
        },
        ...
      }
    ]
}
```

6. Create the token for the service account using the following command:

```
$ kubectl create token api-call -n t23
eyJhbGciOiJSUzI1NiIsImtpZCI6IjBtQkJzJzVWlsQjl...
```

Change the existing Pod definition by deleting and recreating the live object. Add the attribute that disables automounting the token, as shown in the following:

```
apiVersion: v1
kind: Pod
metadata:
  name: service-list
  namespace: t23
spec:
  serviceAccountName: api-call
  automountServiceAccountToken: false
  containers:
  - name: service-list
    image: alpine/curl:3.14
    command: ['sh', '-c', 'while true; do curl -s -k -m 5 \
              -H "Authorization: Bearer eyJhbGciOiJSUzI1NiIsImtpZCI6IjBtQkBzJzVWlsQjl \
              BtQkJzVWlsQjl" https://kubernetes.default.svc.cluster. \
              local/api/v1/namespaces/default/services; sleep 10; \
              done']
```

The API server will allow the HTTPS request performed with the token of the service account to be authenticated and authorized:

```
$ kubectl logs service-list -n t23
{
  "kind": "ServiceList",
  "apiVersion": "v1",
  "metadata": {
    "resourceVersion": "81194"
  },
  "items": [
    {
      "metadata": {
        "name": "kubernetes",
        "namespace": "default",
        "uid": "30eb5425-8f60-4bb7-8331-f91fe0999e20",
        "resourceVersion": "199",
        "creationTimestamp": "2022-09-08T18:06:52Z",
        "labels": {
          "component": "apiserver",
          "provider": "kubernetes"
        },
        ...
      }
    ]
}
```

7. The solution to this sample exercise requires a lot of manual steps. The following commands do not render their output.

Open an interactive shell to the control plane node using Vagrant:

```
$ vagrant ssh kube-control-plane
```

Upgrade kubeadm to version 1.26.1 and apply it:

```
$ sudo apt-mark unhold kubeadm && sudo apt-get update && sudo apt-get \
  install -y kubeadm=1.26.1-00 && sudo apt-mark hold kubeadm
$ sudo kubeadm upgrade apply v1.26.1
```

Drain the node, upgrade the kubelet and kubectl, restart the kubelet, and uncordon the node:

```
$ kubectl drain kube-control-plane --ignore-daemonsets
$ sudo apt-get update && sudo apt-get install -y \
  --allow-change-held-packages kubelet=1.26.1-00 kubectl=1.26.1-00
$ sudo systemctl daemon-reload
$ sudo systemctl restart kubelet
$ kubectl uncordon kube-control-plane
```

The version of the node should now say v1.26.1. Exit the node:

```
$ kubectl get nodes
$ exit
```

Open an interactive shell to the first worker node using Vagrant. Repeat all of the following steps for the worker node:

```
$ vagrant ssh kube-worker-1
```

Upgrade kubeadm to version 1.26.1 and apply it to the node:

```
$ sudo apt-get update && sudo apt-get install -y \
  --allow-change-held-packages kubeadm=1.26.1-00
$ sudo kubeadm upgrade node
```

Drain the node, upgrade the kubelet and kubectl, restart the kubelet, and uncordon the node:

```
$ kubectl drain kube-worker-1 --ignore-daemonsets
$ sudo apt-get update && sudo apt-get install -y \
  --allow-change-held-packages kubelet=1.26.1-00 kubectl=1.26.1-00
$ sudo systemctl daemon-reload
$ sudo systemctl restart kubelet
$ kubectl uncordon kube-worker-1
```

The version of the node should now say v1.26.1. Exit out of the node:

```
$ kubectl get nodes
$ exit
```

Chapter 4, "System Hardening"

1. Shell into the worker node with the following command:

```
$ vagrant ssh kube-worker-1
```

Identify the process exposing port 21. One way to do this is by using the lsof command. The command that exposes the port is vsftpd:

```
$ sudo lsof -i :21
COMMAND   PID USER   FD   TYPE DEVICE SIZE/OFF NODE NAME
vsftpd  10178 root    3u  IPv6  56850      0t0  TCP *:ftp (LISTEN)
```

Alternatively, you could also use the ss command, as shown in the following:

```
$ sudo ss -at -pn '( dport = :21 or sport = :21 )'
State   Recv-Q   Send-Q   Local Address:Port \
   Peer Address:Port   Process
LISTEN  0        32       *:21 \
   *:*   users:(("vsftpd",pid=10178,fd=3))
```

The process vsftpd has been started as a service:

```
$ sudo systemctl status vsftpd
• vsftpd.service - vsftpd FTP server
     Loaded: loaded (/lib/systemd/system/vsftpd.service; enabled; \
             vendor preset: enabled)
     Active: active (running) since Thu 2022-10-06 14:39:12 UTC; \
```

```
                11min ago
   Main PID: 10178 (vsftpd)
      Tasks: 1 (limit: 1131)
     Memory: 604.0K
     CGroup: /system.slice/vsftpd.service
             └─10178 /usr/sbin/vsftpd /etc/vsftpd.conf

  Oct 06 14:39:12 kube-worker-1 systemd[1]: Starting vsftpd FTP server...
  Oct 06 14:39:12 kube-worker-1 systemd[1]: Started vsftpd FTP server.
```

Shut down the service and deinstall the package:

```
$ sudo systemctl stop vsftpd
$ sudo systemctl disable vsftpd
$ sudo apt purge --auto-remove -y vsftpd
```

Checking on the port, you will see that it is not listed anymore:

```
$ sudo lsof -i :21
```

Exit out of the node:

```
$ exit
```

2. Shell into the worker node with the following command:

```
$ vagrant ssh kube-worker-1
```

Create the AppArmor profile at /etc/apparmor.d/network-deny using the command sudo vim /etc/apparmor.d/network-deny. The contents of the file should look as follows:

```
#include <tunables/global>

profile network-deny flags=(attach_disconnected) {
  #include <abstractions/base>

  network,
}
```

Enforce the AppArmor profile by running the following command:

```
$ sudo apparmor_parser /etc/apparmor.d/network-deny
```

You cannot modify the existing Pod object in order to add the annotation for AppArmor. You will need to delete the object first. Write the definition of the Pod to a file:

```
$ kubectl get pod -o yaml > pod.yaml
$ kubectl delete pod network-call
```

Edit the pod.yaml file to add the AppArmor annotation. For the relevant annotation, use the name of the container network-call as part of the key suffix and localhost/network-deny as the value. The suffix network-deny refers to the

name of the AppArmor profile. The final content could look as follows after a
little bit of cleanup:

```
apiVersion: v1
kind: Pod
metadata:
  name: network-call
  annotations:
    container.apparmor.security.beta.kubernetes.io/network-call: \
    localhost/network-deny
spec:
  containers:
  - name: network-call
    image: alpine/curl:3.14
    command: ["sh", "-c", "while true; do ping -c 1 google.com; \
              sleep 5; done"]
```

Create the Pod from the manifest. After a couple of seconds, the Pod should
transition into the "Running" status:

```
$ kubectl create -f pod.yaml
$ kubectl get pod network-call
NAME            READY   STATUS    RESTARTS   AGE
network-call    1/1     Running   0          27s
```

AppArmor prevents the Pod from making a network call. You can check the logs
to verify:

```
$ kubectl logs network-call
...
sh: ping: Permission denied
sh: sleep: Permission denied
```

Exit out of the node:

```
$ exit
```

3. Shell into the worker node with the following command:

```
$ vagrant ssh kube-worker-1
```

Create the target directory for the seccomp profiles:

```
$ sudo mkdir -p /var/lib/kubelet/seccomp/profiles
```

Add the file audit.json in the directory /var/lib/kubelet/seccomp/profiles
with the following content:

```
{
    "defaultAction": "SCMP_ACT_LOG"
}
```

You cannot modify the existing Pod object in order to add the seccomp configuration via the security context. You will need to delete the object first. Write the
definition of the Pod to a file:

```
$ kubectl get pod -o yaml > pod.yaml
$ kubectl delete pod network-call
```

Edit the `pod.yaml` file. Point the seccomp profile to the definition. The final content could look as follows after a little bit of cleanup:

```
apiVersion: v1
kind: Pod
metadata:
  name: network-call
spec:
  securityContext:
    seccompProfile:
      type: Localhost
      localhostProfile: profiles/audit.json
  containers:
  - name: network-call
    image: alpine/curl:3.14
    command: ["sh", "-c", "while true; do ping -c 1 google.com; \
              sleep 5; done"]
    securityContext:
      allowPrivilegeEscalation: false
```

Create the Pod from the manifest. After a couple of seconds, the Pod should transition into the "Running" status:

```
$ kubectl create -f pod.yaml
$ kubectl get pod network-call
NAME           READY   STATUS    RESTARTS   AGE
network-call   1/1     Running   0          27s
```

You should be able to find log entries for syscalls, e.g., for the `sleep` command:

```
$ sudo cat /var/log/syslog
Oct  6 16:25:06 ubuntu-focal kernel: [ 2114.894122] audit: type=1326 \
audit(1665073506.099:23761): auid=4294967295 uid=0 gid=0 \
ses=4294967295 pid=19226 comm="sleep" exe="/bin/busybox" \
sig=0 arch=c000003e syscall=231 compat=0 ip=0x7fc026adbf0b \
code=0x7ffc0000
```

Exit out of the node:

```
$ exit
```

Create the Pod definition in the file `pod.yaml`:

```
apiVersion: v1
kind: Pod
metadata:
  name: sysctl-pod
spec:
  securityContext:
    sysctls:
    - name: net.core.somaxconn
```

```
    value: "1024"
  - name: debug.iotrace
    value: "1"
containers:
- name: nginx
  image: nginx:1.23.1
```

Create the Pod and then check on the status. You will see that the status is "SysctlForbidden":

```
$ kubectl create -f pod.yaml
$ kubectl get pods
NAME          READY   STATUS          RESTARTS   AGE
sysctl-pod    0/1     SysctlForbidden 0          4s
```

The event log will tell you more about the reasoning:

```
$ kubectl describe pod sysctl-pod
...
Events:
  Type     Reason           Age     From     \
           Message
  ----     ------           ----    ----     \
           -------
  Warning  SysctlForbidden  2m48s   kubelet \
           forbidden sysctl: "net.core.somaxconn" \
           not allowlisted
```

Chapter 5, "Minimize Microservice Vulnerabilities"

1. Define the Pod with the security settings in the file busybox-security-context.yaml. You can find the content of the following YAML manifest:

```
apiVersion: v1
kind: Pod
metadata:
  name: busybox-security-context
spec:
  securityContext:
    runAsUser: 1000
    runAsGroup: 3000
    fsGroup: 2000
  volumes:
  - name: vol
    emptyDir: {}
  containers:
  - name: busybox
    image: busybox:1.28
    command: ["sh", "-c", "sleep 1h"]
    volumeMounts:
    - name: vol
```

```
      mountPath: /data/test
    securityContext:
      allowPrivilegeEscalation: false
```
Create the Pod with the following command:

```
$ kubectl apply -f busybox-security-context.yaml
$ kubectl get pod busybox-security-context
NAME                        READY   STATUS    RESTARTS   AGE
busybox-security-context    1/1     Running   0          54s
```

Shell into the container and create the file. You will find that the file group is 2000, as defined by the security context:

```
$ kubectl exec busybox-security-context -it -- /bin/sh
/ $ cd /data/test
/data/test $ touch hello.txt
/data/test $ ls -l
total 0
-rw-r--r--    1 1000     2000            0 Nov 21 18:29 hello.txt
/data/test $ exit
```

2. Specify the namespace named audited in the file psa-namespace.yaml. Set the PSA label with baseline level and the warn mode:

```
apiVersion: v1
kind: Namespace
metadata:
  name: audited
  labels:
    pod-security.kubernetes.io/warn: baseline
```

Create the namespace from the YAML manifest:

```
$ kubectl apply -f psa-namespace.yaml
```

You can produce an error by using the following Pod configuration in the file psa-pod.yaml. The YAML manifest sets the attribute hostNetwork: true, which is not allowed for the baseline level (*https://oreil.ly/c8JEW*):

```
apiVersion: v1
kind: Pod
metadata:
  name: busybox
  namespace: audited
spec:
  hostNetwork: true
  containers:
  - name: busybox
    image: busybox:1.28
    command: ["sh", "-c", "sleep 1h"]
```

Creating the Pod renders a warning message. The Pod will have been created nevertheless. You can prevent the creation of the Pod by configuring the PSA with the restricted level:

```
$ kubectl apply -f psa-pod.yaml
Warning: would violate PodSecurity "baseline:latest": host namespaces \
(hostNetwork=true)
pod/busybox created
$ kubectl get pod busybox -n audited
NAME       READY   STATUS    RESTARTS   AGE
busybox    1/1     Running   0          2m21s
```

3. You can install Gatekeeper with the following command:

```
$ kubectl apply -f https://raw.githubusercontent.com/open-policy-agent/\
gatekeeper/master/deploy/gatekeeper.yaml
```

The Gatekeeper library describes a ConstraintTemplate for defining replica limits (*https://oreil.ly/gyD1-*). Inspect the YAML manifest described on the page. Apply the manifest with the following command:

```
$ kubectl apply -f https://raw.githubusercontent.com/open-policy-agent/\
gatekeeper-library/master/library/general/replicalimits/template.yaml
```

Now, define the Constraint with the YAML manifest in the file named replica-limits-constraint.yaml:

```
apiVersion: constraints.gatekeeper.sh/v1beta1
kind: K8sReplicaLimits
metadata:
  name: replica-limits
spec:
  match:
    kinds:
      - apiGroups: ["apps"]
        kinds: ["Deployment"]
  parameters:
    ranges:
    - min_replicas: 3
      max_replicas: 10
```

Create the Constraint with the following command:

```
$ kubectl apply -f replica-limits-constraint.yaml
```

You can see that a Deployment can only be created if the provided number of replicas falls within the range of the Constraint:

```
$ kubectl create deployment nginx --image=nginx:1.23.2 --replicas=15
error: failed to create deployment: admission webhook \
"validation.gatekeeper.sh" denied the request: [replica-limits] \
The provided number of replicas is not allowed for deployment: nginx. \
Allowed ranges: {"ranges": [{"max_replicas": 10, "min_replicas": 3}]}
```

```
$ kubectl create deployment nginx --image=nginx:1.23.2 --replicas=7
deployment.apps/nginx created
```

4. Configure encryption for etcd, as described in "Encrypting etcd Data" on page 101. Next, create a new Secret with the following imperative command:

```
$ kubectl create secret generic db-credentials \
  --from-literal=api-key=YZvkiWUkycvspyGHk3fQRAkt
```

You can check the encrypted value of the Secret stored in etcd with the following command:

```
$ sudo ETCDCTL_API=3 etcdctl --cacert=/etc/kubernetes/pki/etcd/ca.crt \
--cert=/etc/kubernetes/pki/etcd/server.crt --key=/etc/kubernetes/pki/\
etcd/server.key get /registry/secrets/default/db-credentials | hexdump -C
```

5. Open an interactive shell to the worker node using Vagrant:

```
$ vagrant ssh kube-worker-1
```

Define the RuntimeClass with the following YAML manifest. The contents have been stored in the file runtime-class.yaml:

```
apiVersion: node.k8s.io/v1
kind: RuntimeClass
metadata:
  name: container-runtime-sandbox
handler: runsc
```

Create the RuntimeClass object:

```
$ kubectl apply -f runtime-class.yaml
```

Assign the name of the RuntimeClass to the Pod using the spec.runtimeClass Name attribute. The nginx Pod has been defined in the file pod.yaml:

```
apiVersion: v1
kind: Pod
metadata:
  name: nginx
spec:
  runtimeClassName: container-runtime-sandbox
  containers:
  - name: nginx
    image: nginx:1.23.2
```

Create the Pod object. The Pod will transition into the status "Running":

```
$ kubectl apply -f pod.yaml
$ kubectl get pod nginx
NAME    READY   STATUS    RESTARTS   AGE
nginx   1/1     Running   0          2m21s
```

Exit out of the node:

```
$ exit
```

Chapter 6, "Supply Chain Security"

1. The initial container image built with the provided Dockerfile has a size of 998MB. You can produce and run the container image with the following commands. Run a quick `curl` command to see if the endpoint exposed by the application can be reached:

```
$ docker build . -t node-app:0.0.1
...
$ docker images
REPOSITORY    TAG      IMAGE ID        CREATED         SIZE
node-app      0.0.1    7ba99d4ba3af    3 seconds ago   998MB
$ docker run -p 3001:3001 -d node-app:0.0.1
c0c8a301eeb4ac499c22d10399c424e1063944f18fff70ceb5c49c4723af7969
$ curl -L http://localhost:3001/
Hello World
```

One of the changes you can make is to avoid using a large base image. You could replace it with the `alpine` version of the node base image. Also, avoid pulling the `latest` image. Pick the Node.js version you actually want the application to run with. The following command uses a Dockerfile with the base image `node:19-alpine`, which reduces the container image size to 176MB:

```
$ docker build . -t node-app:0.0.1
...
$ docker images
REPOSITORY    TAG      IMAGE ID        CREATED         SIZE
node-app      0.0.1    ef2fbec41a75    2 seconds ago   176MB
```

2. You can install Kyverno using Helm or by pointing to the YAML manifest available on the project's GitHub repository. We'll use the YAML manifest here:

```
$ kubectl create -f https://raw.githubusercontent.com/kyverno/\
kyverno/main/config/install.yaml
```

Set up a YAML manifest file named `restrict-image-registries.yaml`. Add the following contents to the file. The manifest represents a ClusterPolicy that only allows the use of container images that start with `gcr.io/`. Make sure to assign the value `Enforce` to the attribute `spec.validationFailureAction`:

```
apiVersion: kyverno.io/v1
kind: ClusterPolicy
metadata:
  name: restrict-image-registries
  annotations:
    policies.kyverno.io/title: Restrict Image Registries
    policies.kyverno.io/category: Best Practices, EKS Best Practices
    policies.kyverno.io/severity: medium
    policies.kyverno.io/minversion: 1.6.0
    policies.kyverno.io/subject: Pod
```

```
    policies.kyverno.io/description: >-
      Images from unknown, public registries can be of dubious quality \
      and may not be scanned and secured, representing a high degree of \
      risk. Requiring use of known, approved registries helps reduce \
      threat exposure by ensuring image pulls only come from them. This \
      policy validates that container images only originate from the \
      registry `eu.foo.io` or `bar.io`. Use of this policy requires \
      customization to define your allowable registries.
  spec:
    validationFailureAction: Enforce
    background: true
    rules:
    - name: validate-registries
      match:
        any:
        - resources:
            kinds:
            - Pod
      validate:
        message: "Unknown image registry."
        pattern:
          spec:
            containers:
            - image: "gcr.io/*"
```

Apply the manifest with the following command:

```
$ kubectl apply -f restrict-image-registries.yaml
```

Run the following commands to verify that the policy has become active. Any container image definition that doesn't use the prefix gcr.io/ will be denied:

```
$ kubectl run nginx --image=nginx:1.23.3
Error from server: admission webhook "validate.kyverno.svc-fail" \
denied the request:

policy Pod/default/nginx for resource violation:

restrict-image-registries:
  validate-registries: 'validation error: Unknown image registry. \
  rule validate-registries
    failed at path /spec/containers/0/image/'
$ kubectl run busybox --image=gcr.io/google-containers/busybox:1.27.2
pod/busybox created
```

3. Find the SHA256 hash for the image nginx:1.23.3-alpine with the search functionality of Docker Hub. The search result (*https://oreil.ly/a4o8E*) will lead you to the tag of the image. On top of the page, you should find the digest sha256:c1b9fe3c0c015486cf1e4a0ecabe78d05864475e279638e9713eb55f013f9 07f. Use the digest instead of the tag in the Pod definition. The result is the following YAML manifest:

```
apiVersion: v1
kind: Pod
metadata:
  name: nginx
spec:
  containers:
  - name: nginx
    image: nginx@sha256:c1b9fe3c0c015486cf1e4a0ecabe78d05864475e279638 \
          e9713eb55f013f907f
```

The creation of the Pod should work:

```
$ kubectl apply -f pod-validate-image.yaml
pod/nginx created
$ kubectl get pods nginx
NAME    READY   STATUS    RESTARTS   AGE
nginx   1/1     Running   0          29s
```

If you modify the SHA256 hash in any form and try to recreate the Pod, then Kubernetes would not allow you to pull the image.

4. Running Kubesec in a Docker container results in a whole bunch of suggestions, as shown in the following output:

```
$ docker run -i kubesec/kubesec:512c5e0 scan /dev/stdin < pod.yaml
[
  {
    "object": "Pod/hello-world.default",
    "valid": true,
    "message": "Passed with a score of 0 points",
    "score": 0,
    "scoring": {
      "advise": [
        {
          "selector": "containers[] .securityContext .capabilities \
                      .drop | index(\"ALL\")",
          "reason": "Drop all capabilities and add only those \
                    required to reduce syscall attack surface"
        },
        {
          "selector": "containers[] .resources .requests .cpu",
          "reason": "Enforcing CPU requests aids a fair balancing \
                    of resources across the cluster"
        },
        {
          "selector": "containers[] .securityContext .runAsNonRoot \
                      == true",
          "reason": "Force the running image to run as a non-root \
                    user to ensure least privilege"
        },
        {
          "selector": "containers[] .resources .limits .cpu",
```

```
          "reason": "Enforcing CPU limits prevents DOS via resource \
                     exhaustion"
      },
      {
        "selector": "containers[] .securityContext .capabilities \
                     .drop",
        "reason": "Reducing kernel capabilities available to a \
                   container limits its attack surface"
      },
      {
        "selector": "containers[] .resources .requests .memory",
        "reason": "Enforcing memory requests aids a fair balancing \
                   of resources across the cluster"
      },
      {
        "selector": "containers[] .resources .limits .memory",
        "reason": "Enforcing memory limits prevents DOS via resource \
                   exhaustion"
      },
      {
        "selector": "containers[] .securityContext \
                     .readOnlyRootFilesystem == true",
        "reason": "An immutable root filesystem can prevent malicious \
                   binaries being added to PATH and increase attack \
                   cost"
      },
      {
        "selector": ".metadata .annotations .\"container.seccomp. \
                     security.alpha.kubernetes.io/pod\"",
        "reason": "Seccomp profiles set minimum privilege and secure \
                   against unknown threats"
      },
      {
        "selector": ".metadata .annotations .\"container.apparmor. \
                     security.beta.kubernetes.io/nginx\"",
        "reason": "Well defined AppArmor policies may provide greater \
                   protection from unknown threats. WARNING: NOT \
                   PRODUCTION READY"
      },
      {
        "selector": "containers[] .securityContext .runAsUser -gt \
                     10000",
        "reason": "Run as a high-UID user to avoid conflicts with \
                   the host's user table"
      },
      {
        "selector": ".spec .serviceAccountName",
        "reason": "Service accounts restrict Kubernetes API access \
                   and should be configured with least privilege"
      }
}
```

```
      ]
    }
  }
]
```

The fixed-up YAML manifest could look like this:

```yaml
apiVersion: v1
kind: Pod
metadata:
  name: hello-world
spec:
  serviceAccountName: default
  containers:
  - name: linux
    image: hello-world:linux
    resources:
      requests:
        memory: "64Mi"
        cpu: "250m"
      limits:
        memory: "128Mi"
        cpu: "500m"
    securityContext:
      readOnlyRootFilesystem: true
      runAsNonRoot: true
      runAsUser: 20000
      capabilities:
        drop: ["ALL"]
```

5. Executing the kubectl apply command against the existing setup.yaml manifest will create the Pods named backend, loop, and logstash in the namespace r61:

```
$ kubectl apply -f setup.yaml
namespace/r61 created
pod/backend created
pod/loop created
pod/logstash created
```

You can check on them with the following command:

```
$ kubectl get pods -n r61
NAME        READY   STATUS    RESTARTS   AGE
backend     1/1     Running   0          115s
logstash    1/1     Running   0          115s
loop        1/1     Running   0          115s
```

Check the images of each Pod in the namespace r61 using the kubectl describe command. The images used are bmuschko/nodejs-hello-world:1.0.0, alpine:3.13.4, and elastic/logstash:7.13.3:

```
$ kubectl describe pod backend -n r61
...
Containers:
  hello:
    Container ID:    docker://eb0bdefc75e635d03b625140d1e \
                     b229ca2db7904e44787882147921c2bd9c365
    Image:           bmuschko/nodejs-hello-world:1.0.0
    ...
```

Use the Trivy executable to check vulnerabilities for all images:

```
$ trivy image bmuschko/nodejs-hello-world:1.0.0
$ trivy image alpine:3.13.4
$ trivy image elastic/logstash:7.13.3
```

If you look closely at the list of vulnerabilities, you will find that all images contain issues with "CRITICAL" severity. As a result, delete all Pods:

```
$ kubectl delete pod backend -n r61
$ kubectl delete pod logstash -n r61
$ kubectl delete pod loop -n r61
```

Chapter 7, "Monitoring, Logging, and Runtime Security"

1. Shell into the worker node with the following command:

```
$ vagrant ssh kube-worker-1
```

Inspect the command and arguments of the running Pod named malicious. You will see that it tries to append a message to the file /etc/threat:

```
$ kubectl get pod malicious -o jsonpath='{.spec.containers[0].args}'
...
spec:
  containers:
  - args:
    - /bin/sh
    - -c
    - while true; do echo "attacker intrusion" >> /etc/threat; \
      sleep 5; done
...
```

One of Falco's default rules monitors file operations that try to write to the /etc directory. You can find a message for every write attempt in standard output:

```
$ sudo journalctl -fu falco
Jan 24 23:40:18 kube-worker-1 falco[8575]: 23:40:18.359740123: Error \
File below /etc opened for writing (user=<NA> user_loginuid=-1 \
command=sh -c while true; do echo "attacker intrusion" >> /etc/threat; \
sleep 5; done pid=9763 parent=<NA> pcmdline=<NA> file=/etc/threat \
program=sh gparent=<NA> ggparent=<NA> gggparent=<NA> \
```

```
container_id=e72a6dbb63b8 image=docker.io/library/alpine)
...
```

Find the rule that produces the message in `/etc/falco/falco_rules.yaml` by searching for the string "etc opened for writing." The rule looks as follows:

```
- rule: Write below etc
  desc: an attempt to write to any file below /etc
  condition: write_etc_common
  output: "File below /etc opened for writing (user=%user.name \
          user_loginuid=%user.loginuid command=%proc.cmdline \
          pid=%proc.pid parent=%proc.pname pcmdline=%proc.pcmdline \
          file=%fd.name program=%proc.name gparent=%proc.aname[2] \
          ggparent=%proc.aname[3] gggparent=%proc.aname[4] \
          container_id=%container.id image=%container.image.repository)"
  priority: ERROR
  tags: [filesystem, mitre_persistence]
```

Copy the rule to the file `/etc/falco/falco_rules.local.yaml` and modify the output definition, as follows:

```
- rule: Write below etc
  desc: an attempt to write to any file below /etc
  condition: write_etc_common
  output: "%evt.time,%user.name,%container.id"
  priority: ERROR
  tags: [filesystem, mitre_persistence]
```

Restart the Falco service, and find the changed output in the Falco logs:

```
$ sudo systemctl restart falco
$ sudo journalctl -fu falco
Jan 24 23:48:18 kube-worker-1 falco[17488]: 23:48:18.516903001: \
Error 23:48:18.516903001,<NA>,e72a6dbb63b8
...
```

Edit the file `/etc/falco/falco.yaml` to change the output channel. Disable standard output, enable file output, and point the `file_output` attribute to the file `/var/log/falco.log`. The resulting configuration will look like the following:

```
file_output:
  enabled: true
  keep_alive: false
  filename: /var/log/falco.log

stdout_output:
  enabled: false
```

The log file will now append Falco log:

```
$ sudo tail -f /var/log/falco.log
00:10:30.425084165: Error 00:10:30.425084165,<NA>,e72a6dbb63b8
...
```

Exit out of the VM:

```
$ exit
```

2. Create the Pod named hash from the setup.yaml file. The command running in its container appends a hash to a file at /var/config/hash.txt in an infinite loop:

```
$ kubectl apply -f setup.yaml
pod/hash created
$ kubectl get pod hash
NAME    READY   STATUS    RESTARTS   AGE
hash    1/1     Running   0          27s
$ kubectl exec -it hash -- /bin/sh
/ # ls /var/config/hash.txt
/var/config/hash.txt
```

To make the container immutable, you will have to add configuration to the existing Pod definition. You have to set the root filesystem to read-only access and mount a Volume to the path /var/config to allow writing to the file named hash.txt. The resulting YAML manifest could look as follows:

```
apiVersion: v1
kind: Pod
metadata:
  name: hash
spec:
  containers:
  - name: hash
    image: alpine:3.17.1
    securityContext:
      readOnlyRootFilesystem: true
    volumeMounts:
    - name: hash-vol
      mountPath: /var/config
    command: ["sh", "-c", "if [ ! -d /var/config ]; then mkdir -p \
             /var/config; fi; while true; do echo $RANDOM | md5sum \
             | head -c 20 >> /var/config/hash.txt; sleep 20; done"]
  volumes:
  - name: hash-vol
    emptyDir: {}
```

3. Shell into the control plane node with the following command:

```
$ vagrant ssh kube-control-plane
```

Edit the existing audit policy file at /etc/kubernetes/audit/rules/audit-policy.yaml. Add the rules asked about in the instructions. The content of the final audit policy file could look as follows:

```
apiVersion: audit.k8s.io/v1
kind: Policy
omitStages:
  - "RequestReceived"
rules:
  - level: RequestResponse
    resources:
    - group: ""
      resources: ["pods"]
  - level: Metadata
    resources:
    - group: ""
      resources: ["secrets", "configmaps"]
  - level: Request
    resources:
    - group: ""
      resources: ["services"]
```

Configure the API server to consume the audit policy file by editing the file /etc/kubernetes/manifests/kube-apiserver.yaml. Provide additional options, as requested. The relevant configuration needed is as follows:

```
...
spec:
  containers:
  - command:
    - kube-apiserver
    - --audit-policy-file=/etc/kubernetes/audit/rules/audit-policy.yaml
    - --audit-log-path=/var/log/kubernetes/audit/logs/apiserver.log
    - --audit-log-maxage=5
    ...
    volumeMounts:
    - mountPath: /etc/kubernetes/audit/rules/audit-policy.yaml
      name: audit
      readOnly: true
    - mountPath: /var/log/kubernetes/audit/logs/
      name: audit-log
      readOnly: false
    ...
  volumes:
  - name: audit
    hostPath:
      path: /etc/kubernetes/audit/rules/audit-policy.yaml
      type: File
  - name: audit-log
    hostPath:
```

```
    path: /var/log/kubernetes/audit/logs/
    type: DirectoryOrCreate
```

One of the logged resources is a ConfigMap on the `Metadata` level. The following command creates an exemplary ConfigMap object:

```
$ kubectl create configmap db-user --from-literal=username=tom
configmap/db-user created
```

The audit log file will now contain an entry for the event:

```
$ sudo cat /var/log/kubernetes/audit/logs/apiserver.log
{"kind":"Event","apiVersion":"audit.k8s.io/v1","level":"Metadata", \
"auditID":"1fbb409a-3815-4da8-8a5e-d71c728b98b1","stage": \
"ResponseComplete","requestURI":"/api/v1/namespaces/default/configmaps? \
fieldManager=kubectl-create\u0026fieldValidation=Strict","verb": \
"create","user":{"username":"kubernetes-admin","groups": \
["system:masters","system:authenticated"]},"sourceIPs": \
["192.168.56.10"], "userAgent":"kubectl/v1.24.4 (linux/amd64) \
kubernetes/95ee5ab", "objectRef":{"resource":"configmaps", \
"namespace":"default", "name":"db-user","apiVersion":"v1"}, \
"responseStatus":{"metadata": {},"code":201}, \
"requestReceivedTimestamp":"2023-01-25T18:57:51.367219Z", \
"stageTimestamp":"2023-01-25T18:57:51.372094Z","annotations": \
{"authorization.k8s.io/decision":"allow", \
"authorization.k8s.io/reason":""}}
```

Exit out of the VM:

```
$ exit
```

Index

attacker can call API Server from Internet, 48

attacker can call API Server from Service Account, 52

attacker exploits container vulnerabilities, 114

attacker exploits package vulnerabilities, 66

attacker gains access to another container, 104

attacker gains access to Dashboard functionality, 31

attacker gains access to node running etcd, 99

attacker gains access to pods, 12

attacker injects malicious code into binary, 37

attacker injects malicious code into container images, 119

attacker installs malicious software, 151

attacker listens to communication between two pods, 108

attacker misuses root user container access, 86

attacker uploads malicious container images, 122

attacker uses credentials to gain file access, 68

compromised Pod accessing metadata servers, 29

developer doesn't follow pod security best practices, 91

Kubernetes administrator can observe actions taken by attackers, 142

seccomp, 7, 79-82

Secrets
about, 151
configuring containers with, 152
creating for service accounts, 58
managing, 99-103

security
enforcing standards for namespaces, 93
fixing issues with, 20
of supply chain, 5
(see also supply chain security)
runtime, 6
setting OS-level domains, 85-98

security contexts, 86

SecurityContext API, 86

SELinux (Security-Enhanced Linux), 75

semantic versioning scheme, 59

service account
binding to Pods, 53
creating Secrets for, 58
disabling automounting for tokens, 57
expiration of token, 34
generating tokens, 58
minimizing permissions for, 53-59

ServiceAccount, 33

services, disabling, 66

SHA, 38

SHA256, 39, 120

signing container images, 119

size, of base images, 114

snapd package manager, 66

ss command, 73

static analysis, of workload, 130-134

status command, 67

Study4exam, 8

su command, 70

sudo command, 70

sudo systemctl restart kubelet command, 129

supply chain security, 113-138
about, 5, 113
answers to review questions, 178-183
minimizing base image footprint, 113-119
sample exercises, 138
scanning images for known vulnerabilities, 135
securing supply chain, 119-130
static analysis of workload, 130-134

sysctl command, 90

system hardening, 65-83
about, 5, 65
answers to review questions, 170-174
minimizing external access to networks, 73
minimizing host OS footprint, 65-68
minimizing IAM roles, 68-73
sample exercises, 83
using kernel hardening tools, 75-82

systemctl command, 66

systemctl status command, 74

T

Tetragon, 142

TLS (Transport Layer Security)
creating an ingress with termination, 22-28
creating TLS certificate and key, 25
termination of, 4

About the Author

Benjamin Muschko is a software engineer, consultant, and trainer with more than 20 years of experience in the industry. He's passionate about project automation, testing, and continuous delivery. Ben is an author, a frequent speaker at conferences, and an avid open source advocate. He holds the CKAD, CKA, and CKS certifications and is a CNCF Ambassador Spring 2023.

Software projects sometimes feel like climbing a mountain. In his free time, Ben loves hiking Colorado's 14ers (*https://www.14ers.com*) and enjoys conquering long-distance trails.

Colophon

The animal on the cover of *Certified Kubernetes Security Specialist (CKS) Study Guide* is a domestic goose. These birds have been selectively bred from wild greylag (*Anser anse*) and swan geese (*Anser cygnoides domesticus*). They have been introduced to every continent except Antarctica. Archaeological evidence shows the geese have been domesticated since at least 4,000 years ago.

Wild geese range in size from 7 to 9 pounds, whereas domestic geese have been bred for size and can weigh up to 22 pounds. The distribution of their fat deposits gives the domestic goose a more upright posture compared to the horizontal posture of their wild ancestors. Their larger size also makes them less likely to fly, although the birds are capable of some flight.

Historically, geese have been domesticated for use of their meat, eggs, and feathers. In more recent times, geese have been kept as backyard pets or even for yard maintenance since they eat weeds and leaves. Due to the loud and aggressive nature of geese, they have also been used to safeguard property, since they will make a lot of noise if they perceive a threat or an intruder.

Domestic animals are not assessed by the IUCN. Many of the animals on O'Reilly covers are endangered; all of them are important to the world.

The cover illustration is by Karen Montgomery. The cover fonts are Gilroy Semibold and Guardian Sans. The text font is Adobe Minion Pro; the heading font is Adobe Myriad Condensed; and the code font is Dalton Maag's Ubuntu Mono.

Printed in the USA
CPSIA information can be obtained
at www.ICGtesting.com
JSHW052341250923
49107JS00007B/27

9 781098 132972